OCEANIC NEW YORK

OCEANIC NEW YORK

Edited by
Steve Mentz

*To Arlene,
With thanks —*

[signature]

punctum books ℗ brooklyn, n.y.

OCEANIC NEW YORK
© 2015 Steve Mentz

First published in 2015 by
punctum books
Brooklyn, New York
http://punctumbooks.com

punctum books is an independent, open-access publisher dedicated to radically creative modes of intellectual inquiry and writing across a whimsical para-humantities assemblage. We solicit and pimp quixotic, sagely mad engagements with textual thought-bodies. We provide shelters for intellectual vagabonds.

ISBN-13: 978-0692496916
ISBN-10: 0692496912

Cover: Marina Zurkow.
Facing-page drawing: Heather Masciandaro.
Book design: Chris Piuma.

Before you start to read this book,

take this moment to think about making a donation
to punctum books, an independent non-profit press,

@ http://punctumbooks.com/about/

If you're reading the e-book, you can click on the
image below to go directly to our donations site.
Any amount, no matter the size, is appreciated and
will help us to keep our ship of fools afloat.
Contributions from dedicated readers will also
help us to keep our commons open and to cultivate
new work that can't find a welcoming port elsewhere.
Our adventure is not possible without your support.
Vive la open-access.

Fig. 1. Hieronymus Bosch, *Ship of Fools* (1490-1500)

Contents

Instructions: How to Use this Book
Connecting Poem: Asymmetrical Kicking

I. Salt-Water City

Connecting Poem: Two Sublimes

II. The Water is Rising

Instructions
How to Use This Book

Steve Mentz

13 I don't imagine you need any rudimentary
teaching in how to use a technology like the
one in your hands right now. Books are familiar,
whether they comprise sheets of paper bound
and glued or pixels on a screen. But I'm going to
ask you to operate this one differently. I want
you, with this object in your hands, to imagine
that these pages contain the Ocean and New
York City. That makes it a three-fold artifact,
Ocean and City and Book.

12 If this Book were Ocean, how would it feel
between your fingers? Wet and slippery, just a
bit warmer or colder than the air around it, since
the Ocean is our planet's greatest reservoir of
heat, a sloshing insulator and incubator girdling
our globe. Oceans splash alongside Cities and
continents. Perhaps you think that a Book can't
be an Ocean because the property of the first
thing is that we can read it, and the property of
the second is that it is too vast for comprehen-

sion. But I'm asking that we try. There must be a way to read the Ocean!

11   New York City is a different sort of creature. With its concrete exoskeleton always visible, it strains upwards, redolent with human struggles. For those of us who grew up in the shadow of its towers, it's the City that defines modern America. Money and art and office-buildings and every kind of performance culture crowd the pavement, spill into the boroughs, leave smoky traces in the air. Home of Jay Z, Emma Goldman, and Hart Crane, it's a place with a hidden heart.

10   What if all of these things were one thing? All together: this Book and the Ocean and New York City? In the long historical pause between the day the last sailing ship docked at South Street and the day Hurricane Sandy brought the waves back in fury, the City turned its back on the sea. It's time to remember, as this Book asks us to remember, that New York was founded on the Ocean, peopled by its currents, grew rich on its traffic. The storm taught what we should never have forgotten: under the asphalt lies not beach but Ocean.

9   You hold this tripartite object in your hands, Book-Ocean-City. I want to begin where I always begin, with my favorite sailor, Melville's Ishmael. His story begins *Oceanic New York*. Let's start where he starts in the first chapter of *Moby-Dick*, standing at southern tip of the island, looking

out over the water. When this schoolteacher-
turned-whaleman walked the streets of "your
insular city of the Manhattoes," he knew New
York as oceanic city and commercial capital.
Standing on the Battery, he saw a cityscape
"belted round by wharves as Indian islands by
coral reefs—commerce surrounds it with her
surf." Today commerce dominates but the surf
lies hidden.

8   *Oceanic New York* salvages the City's salt-water
past and present. We take inspiration from
Elizabeth Albert's gorgeous exhibition of historical artifacts and contemporary art, *Silent Beaches,
Untold Stories*, which was on display in Queens
the night our voyage began in September 2013.
Buoyed up by art, we plunged into the urban
and oceanic. "Circumambulate the city of a
dreamy Sabbath afternoon," entices Ishmael.
"Nothing will content [us] but the extremest
limit of the land."

7   The twentieth century witnessed the drying up
of New York. The industrial port fled across
the harbor to Newark, the oyster beds were
exhausted, South Street Seaport became a
museum. The twenty-first century flows the
other way. Ecological crises, extreme storms, and
growing recall of oceanic presence are returning
New York's salt-water identity. This book's essays,
poems, images, and conversations surface the
oceanic strata on which New York floats. *Oceanic
New York* goes beyond insular Manhattoes into

Dead Horse Bay, Newtown Creek, and the Hudson River. It reaches everywhere: wherever salt water seeps into our shoes and stains our clothes.

6   The seventeen contributors to this book were together in September 2013 at St. John's University in Queens, where we gave voice to shared fantasies: that the City can become fluid, and Ocean find a solid place in history. That night's speakers are joined in these pages by members of our audience, writers, students, and professors, who have added their voices to our stream. The results, like New York's waterways, aren't always clear blue. There's plenty of particulate matter in these waters, and the resulting flows can be dense and complex. This book offers itself to you as an assist in stormy waters, like the coffin-life buoy that "shot lengthwise from the sea" in the final moments of *Moby-Dick*, protecting Ishmael-readers from drowning, from sharks, and from birds of prey.

5   My core fantasy hopes that in bringing these things together, the Ocean and New York and a Book, we can think new thoughts on the water's edge, as we wait for the next wave together. I don't have delusions about the power of the humanities to save us. I don't even want to rely on our oldest friend, the one who's been with us since the cave paintings, capital-A Art, to save us. (Most people think Art is a man's name, said a wise New Yorker in a more ecologically innocent time.) But I have hopes for language, ideas,

conversations, and the solidarity they bring, on the oceanic edge of our City.

4   In the pages that follow, I use two pieces of my own poetry to connect the essays of *Oceanic New York*. The first poem, "Asymmetrical Kicking," speaks out of the water in the voice of an object from the *Silent Beaches* exhibition, a doll's leg that was lost in the surf and found much later on the beach in Dead Horse Bay. This poem introduces the first section of short essays, "Salt-Water City," which focus on the oceanic tendrils infiltrating twenty-first century New York. The second connecting poem, "Two Sublimes," thinks through the impact of hurricanes Irene and Sandy on my Connecticut home, barely within commuting distance of the City where I teach. In its effort to aestheticize disaster, this poem introduces the second section, "The Water is Rising," which expands oceanic thinking into the vast geographies extending from New York. The essays in this section explore global histories and the more abstract realms of metaphor and phenomenology.

3   The book's final words splash outward into the cold waters of the Irish Sea near Dublin, by way of four "swim poems" and a photograph. These poems end this book with an effort to reach from New York into global waters. The poems respond to a photograph by the immersive artist Vanessa Daws as an incitement to consider the stories of immersion and oceanic awareness that this book

contains. What happens to us, these poems ask, when we turn from land to sea?

2   To be in the Ocean with these poems means leaving the City, at least for a while. But if you use this Book well, and it works the way I hope it can, you'll know that City and Ocean are spaces that can't be separated, that when we plunge into asphalt grids or salty flows we encounter alien mixtures that unsettle and attract. There may be no final ordering for these environments, no perfect transparency at which we can arrive. In moving between them we acknowledge their connections, and in remembering both we honor their mobility. All Cities touch Seas, and all the world's Oceans lap rapaciously at urban shores.

1   *Oceanic New York* begins with these Instructions, but I hope by the time you make it to the far shore, it ends up creating new ideas.

Asymmetrical Kicking

Steve Mentz

Image 1: "Doll's Leg, Dead Horse Bay."
Digital Photgraph, 2012. Elizabeth Albert.

I knew she'd miss me.
Points of fingers digging slightly,
Varying pressure across my unfeeling thigh,
Holding whatever was around us.
Touch binds emotion to dead things.
It skates along filaments to sinews,
Plastic to skin to salt.
She brought me to the beach, into the surf, out here:
That was her mistake.

Beneath the surface flows another world.
Sideways I kick inside it,
Detached,
Solitary.
Lashing out, I move
Asymmetrically.
No longer attached to body or world or girl,
I swim alone.
The salt burns and trickles inside me,
Filling me up.
A dark motion holds me for a long time.

Returning is another leaving.
Never stepping twice onto the same sand,
Out of the same salt water, alongside the same
Dead things.
Air feels empty after so much water.
Now when I kick nothing moves.

Salt-Water City

The first selection of ten essays splashes into the streets, bays, and beaches of New York City.

More salt water appears there than you might expect.

Elizabeth Albert tells the story of her art exhibition, *Silent Beaches, Untold Stories*, in the company of which Oceanic New York told its tales.

Granville Ganter engages the toxins and aesthetic power of "Miss Newtown Creek" in Long Island City.

Lowell Duckert discovers an Arctic heart in Oceanic New York.

Jamie Skye Bianco sings of "#bottlesNbones" in and around Dead Horse Beach.

Alison Kinney describes a "Groundswell" of activism real and imagined.

Bailey Robertson responds to the precocity of her hometown's entanglement with the sea.

Karl Steel imagines that he (and we) are mostly oysters.

Matt Zazzarino fears the digital ocean.

Nancy Nowacek and Lowell Duckert together write "A Short History of the Hudsonian Ice Age."

Steve Mentz finds "Wages of Water" both in the Hudson River and inside his left ear.

Silent Beaches

Elizabeth Albert

I n the fall of 2013 I curated an exhibition for
St. John's University: *Silent Beaches, Untold Stories:
New York City's Forgotten Waterfront*. The *Silent Beaches*
project initially grew out of the startling realization that I,
a second generation New Yorker, had scant knowledge and
scantier experience of our city's 600-plus miles of coastline.
I resolved to get out there, and began a series of excursions
spaning the next three years. I drove and walked and sometimes found I couldn't even get close to the water—huge
power plants, fenced off brown-fields, private property
guarded by vicious dogs were often in my way. But what I
did see was astonishing: beautiful, hideous, sad, and just
weird. Every plant, every used needle, every wreck, every
proud neighbor told the briny story of Oceanic New York.

The more I explored the watery edges of New York,
the more questions I had. What has changed our relationship to the waterfront? How did resorts become ghettos?
Why are former industrial wastelands now fashionable
and rich? Why have coveted oyster beds become choked
with toxic sludge? Do we desire, loathe, devour, dread the
waterfront?

These questions led me in various directions: to the city's photographic archives, to history and literature, to environmental studies, and to a group of artists whose wonderful work heightens awareness of New York City's coastline and waterways.

The *Silent Beaches, Untold Stories* exhibition was organized around a small handful of sites located throughout the five boroughs. The following passages peer into two of these locations through field notes, photographs, and a bit of history.

College Point, 6/15/11
Williamsburgh Yacht Club

We park and walk. Hot and dusty streets, with nobody around except one auto-mechanic. Shirtless, oil-soaked bandana in pocket, he glances over at us and heads into the garage. We pass rotting bungalows, protected by makeshift scarecrows made from sheets with the eyes cut out. Scare me away, for sure. One little sagging bungalow has a faded For Rent sign; cinderblock chop shops abound. We're looking for the Williamsburgh Yacht Club, a venerable old place, counting William Steinway and the beer baron George Ehret among its original clientele. The yacht club was first located on the Newtown Creek, but moved northeast to escape the spreading industry and accompanying filth, first to Bowery Bay in Astoria, and finally to College Point, where it gave up trying to outrun the muck.

There's a chain link fence with a small new-looking Williamsburgh Yacht Club sign. A larger, brighter sign next to it reads:

CAUTION WET WEATHER DISCHARGE POINT
THIS OUTFALL MAY DISCHARGE RAINWATER
MIXED WITH UNTREATED SEWAGE DURING OR
FOLLOWING RAINFALL AND CAN CONTAIN
BACTERIA THAT CAN CAUSE ILLNESS

Through the fence is a large light blue aluminum hangar-like structure, and what looks like a terrace overlooking a sloping asphalt launch, all enclosed by another chain link fence. To the right of the fence is an overgrown lot, a trashed cuddy cabin nestled in the tall weeds. Peering out of a porthole is a moldy stuffed kitty, one eye missing.

We move on trying not to stare down unpaved driveways at boats propped up on scaffolding being sanded and painted by aging beer-bellied men who look like there's no place they'd rather be and are probably still strong as hell.

College Point, 6/23/11
Buddy's Place

At a dead end we encounter a long wooden fence, about five feet high with a gate whose toprail is carved with "Buddy's Place" and a clover leaf. It all looks freshly stained and urethaned and we practically jump out of our skins from the thud of hurling bodies and the onslaught of furious barking and snarling just on the other side of maybe three inches of pine. We're gasping and a man opens the gate and comes out, quieting the dogs. He asks if we're not from around here. No, we agree, "we're from Brooklyn."

The man is friendly and chatty, and I wish I could remember his name. He tells us that he built the place himself. It's a house sitting on an old barge, partially submerged in the water. It's all dedicated to his dad, a firefighter who lost his life on 9/11. He loved and missed the old man. We talked about the attack and where we all were: a conversation New Yorkers know all too well, but one I hadn't had in years.

> College Point is named for St. Paul's College, which existed from only 1835–1850. Originally farmland, the area was gradually transformed into a lovely water-side recreation area with visitors spilling over from William Steinway's North Beach resort, and hotels and saloons springing up to catch the overflow. As the area developed, many elegant Victorian homes were built, some of which remain on shady streets towards the north.
>
> In 1852, Conrad Poppenhusen, an immigrant from Hamburg, Germany, moved to what was still a rural village to expand his business operation and build one of the first major industrial complexes, the American Hard Rubber Company, which produced the then newly developed vulcanized rubber for Charles Goodyear.[1]

As we were talking I noticed an empty lot next to his place that sloped down to the water. In between the trees some-one had carved out blocks of dirt, creating two steps down to a path made of washed-out planks. I told him about my waterfront project and asked if we could go down to

---

1   Arthur Schlegel, *Schlegel's German-American Families in the United States*, Edition Deluxe, Volume II (New York: The American Historical Society, 1917), 99–105.

the shore through the lot. He said sure but warned us to watch our step. He said it was not unusual for bags of used needles and other hospital refuse to wash up. Once there was a human head. He assured us that it must've floated over from the Bronx.

Between what was clearly dumped and what had washed up, the "beach" was pretty much completely covered with refuse. Here and there a bit of sand would peek out from beneath the hunks of Styrofoam, rotting planks, tangled cables, and just plain old garbage. To the left we could see Buddy's Place sitting on its barge. In the water behind was a half-sunk wooden ship complete with old-fashioned wooden steering wheel, the kind that bulges out at the tips. I thought of Popeye. LaGuardia Airport was just across the bay, the planes coming in loud and low. Out on a pile was a man fishing. A skinny cat streaked across the wreckage, disappearing into the Locust and Sumac. I looked down at a dead turtle perched on end, its eyes dry sockets.

Coney Island Creek, 7/13/11
Calvert Vaux Park

I had read about the ghost ships and the yellow submarine, but couldn't figure out where they were. I had never even heard of Calvert Vaux Park. I was familiar with Vaux's work: Central Park's Greensward's plan, Fort Greene Park, Prospect Park, Morningside Park, among others. I found Calvert Vaux Park on the map. It lay along the Belt Parkway somewhere between the Verrazano Bridge and Coney Island.

We drive past it three times. Back and forth on the crawling Belt, cursing each time we exit, eventually finding

ourselves in a massive Big Box parking lot. We park and
continue on foot, a good thing since the entrance is pretty
much unmarked. There's a tiny sign with a Maple leaf,
mostly covered by poison ivy. Then, one hundred feet or so
away we come upon the entrance gate, boarded up but ajar.
A large sign reads:

WARNING
CONTAMINATED SOIL REMOVAL HAZARD
DO NOT ENTER
UNLESS AUTHORIZED

We slip in and follow a long dusty road littered with
various signs of construction. In the distance two men walk
towards us, fishing tackle in hand. I am too embarrassed
to ask where the ghost ships are, and anyway they speak
Russian and do not acknowledge us. The road becomes
overgrown fields shot through with a few narrow pathways.
We note rusty goal posts demarcating
a soccer field.

College Point, 8/10/12
The Tide and Current Taxi

When I arrive Marie and Suze are already on the beach. I
can see them through the trees hauling Marie's rowboat to
the water. I slip on the mud steps heading down to the gar-
bage-strewn shore. I am beyond excited to get a look at this
strange stretch of coastline from the water. It's a hot bright
late morning in August and I may fry. M takes the bow, S
takes the stern, and I'm in the middle. I'm photographing
like mad. We push off into the scummy water. I get a good
look at Buddy's Place from the side and the crazy old

Popeye half-sunk wreck behind. The shore recedes and I feel a flutter of fear. I've developed a kind of agoraphobia out in the water. Such a bummer for someone who grew up swimming every chance I could get.

A thundering roar overhead and we duck. We're directly under the flight path for planes landing at LaGuardia. We look up at the crackling air in the plane's wake. That plane was really huge and really low. S quotes her boyfriend saying, "how strange is it that we fly!?"

> College Point has a history of aviation. The Flushing Airport was located here and was New York's busiest airport until North Beach Airport, later renamed LaGuardia airport (1939), was expanded just across Flushing Bay. North Beach Airport had enjoyed an earlier incarnation as North Beach resort owned by William Steinway of Steinway pianos. EDO Aircraft Corp., the second oldest aerospace company in the U.S., was founded in a shed here in 1925 by Earl Dodge Osborn, inventor of aluminum floats for seaplanes. Osborn's early designs were used by pioneering aviators Charles Lindbergh, Amelia Earhart and Admiral Richard Byrd.[2]

We follow the shore southward past an old barge flanked with tires. The shoreline is wild scrub and Suze notices whole banks of mugwort. She sounds confident and knowledgeable, the youngest of us three. I learn that mugwort was used in medieval Europe to protect travelers from demons and wild animals.

2   Long Island Technology Hall of Fame, Stony Brook University, NY. Copyright © 2014 Long Island Technology Hall of Fame.

The bay narrows. On the opposite bank is the imposing St. Lawrence Cement Factory. It is huge and loud and prosperous looking. We were thinking we'd go as far as the inlet separating College Point from Elmhurst, but it's blocked off with pilings. We try ducking under a low bridge and encounter a melted computer monitor sitting on a sandbar in the shade. Time to turn around.

Up ahead is the College Point transfer station, its placement a point of much contention. The garbage attracts the birds and the birds collide with the planes and you get the picture. I suddenly remember the strangely terrifying bedsheet scarecrows I saw in the nearby streets. We're back where we started and so head north toward a distant marina.

I'm in the bow and paddling feels good, even sweating in the midday heat. We're far from shore and the water is opaque. I'm really trying not to think about how deep it might be. The wind is calm.

Coney Island Creek, 7/1/12
Ghost Ships

Our path takes a sharp left and I see a shimmering through the trees. We turn and as the path slopes down to the water's edge we encounter a fresh and enormous pile of shit. Has to be human. I step over it, refusing to be put off. We emerge from the trees and there they are, spread out before us, more of them than I had expected. I can make out large wooden hulls, some long and rectangular, perhaps barges, and some very old wooden fishing boats. Everything's rotting and splintered. Huge iron nails and spikes jut out at all angles, moss and slime cover every surface.

Coney Island Creek lies at the southern edge of the little-used Calvert Vaux Park. It was reported that Vaux, the celebrated co-designer of Central Park, became depressed later in life from lack of appreciation of his work. On a foggy evening in November 1895 he visited his son, who lived in the area, went for a walk along Coney Island Creek, and was later found floating. It is unknown whether he took his own life or, disoriented in the fog, lost his balance.

The wrecks are beautiful. I can't believe it. How have I lived in Brooklyn for almost 30 years and never even heard of this place? We stand staring. The more we look, the more we see. Then further out in the water I glimpse the sub. It's pale yellow and rusted through, except its turret, which is relatively intact. I realize that even if we walk all the way out on the largest wreck without slipping on the slime and falling on a spike, we still can't get close enough to it.

One of the stranger sights amongst the strewn wreckage is a small, listing yellowish submarine. Jerry Bianco, a former shipbuilder constructed the *Quester I* from repurposed materials and bargain yellow paint. He planned to find the wreck of the *Andrea Doria* and its unclaimed treasures off the coast of Rhode Island. There were some initial problems, and before they were solved a storm tore the sub from its moorings and lodged it in the mud far from shore. The sub remains glued to the spot, decaying. She never made her maiden voyage.

We climb around. Life is there in the murk. We see a tiny orange crab, looking plump and alive amongst the oily pebbles. Striding across mossy pilings is a fancy wading bird that I later identify as a yellow crowned night heron (belongs, I think, in Florida.) Our next find hadn't made it—a dead baby monkfish, its fang-y visage poking up from the rocks.

We see a guy on the top of a rotted out barge, his fishing line bobbing in the sludge. He tells us he's crabbing. He asks if we had noticed a large homeless encampment further down the shore. A few in the camp had fished out a civil war era cannon not long ago. He wonders how much they got for it. Last summer he heard that a group of Germans had wanted to buy the yellow sub, but the deal fell though. I look across the Creek to see a towering brick apartment complex next to a massive Toys R Us.

Coney Island Creek is the only remaining creek in the vicinity that was not filled in as Brooklyn developed. It was originally a small meandering waterway ending in marshlands. Ambitious plans for transforming the area into a thriving port—a Brooklyn rival to Manhattan's Seaport—inspired Thomas Stillwell, descendant of early landowners in the Coney area, to canalize the creek connecting it with Sheepshead Bay, thereby making what was then Coney Hook into an actual island. When the boroughs consolidated in 1898, the plan was abandoned. By 1929 sections of it were filled in to enable rail and car transportation.

During Prohibition, Coney Island Creek was a frequent stop on Rum Row, a watery pathway for schooners smuggling illegal liquor from Canada, the Caribbean, and Europe. Part of the New York City operation was run by big time mafiosos like Frank Costello, boss of the Luciano crime family; "Big Bill"

Dwyer, one time owner of the Brooklyn Dodgers and other sports teams; Joe Masseria, boss of the Genovese family; and Frankie "the Undertaker" Yale.

Brooklyn Borough Gas leeched pollution into the creek from the 1890s to the 1950s. Excavated debris from the building of the Verrazano Bridge as well as other unmonitored dumping added to the murk. No one knows exactly when the ghost ships began appearing near the mouth of the creek, but local residents remember playing on them in the 1950s when they were still floating. Some of them are said to be old wooden deep sea fishing ships whose owners did not want to pay to have them properly disposed of. They would haul them to the Creek and burn them down to the waterline. The Army Corps of Engineers has identified abandoned ships in other parts of the city, but not here. The creek sludge is so toxic that disturbing the wrecks would release a torrent of dangerous chemicals into the water and air.

College Point, 8/10/12
Party Barge in Deep Decline

The sun's in our eyes and we're rowing against the current towards the Marina. We blink and squint at the impressive array of wrecks. One looks like a very big yacht listing deeply. We puzzle over whether the tall protruding structure is a high dive or some kind of radar. Another appears to be a massive half-sunk crane. We pass other wrecks, and further in, what seem to be seaworthy pleasure and fishing craft.

We leave the marina behind and continue north, planning to turn around before we get to the Tallman Island

Sewage Treatment Plant. In the distance is what looks like
a house sitting out in the water. We're squinting, trying
to make it out. As we get closer it gets stranger: plywood
structure weathered grey, multi-level, a cluster of additions
with a taller, pointed central entrance. White framed
windows on either side are blown out, jagged shards still
in place. The whole left side slumped toward the water.
We pull up to it. The foundation below the grey plywood
is a deep russet iron. M thinks the iron base might be
an old ferry. We tie off and board, stepping gingerly over
rotting planks, snaking wires, holes right through to the
water below. One large room has heaps of rotting furniture, clothing, and big hunks of appliances: an old fridge,
overturned toilets, what may have been a part of a bar.
S holds up a cassette.

Poppenhusen's American Rubber Manufacturing
Company aimed to provide a utopian ideal of work and
life for his employees. His vision included homes and
parks, numerous streets, the First Reformed Church,
and the Poppenhusen Institute. He also is credited with
establishing one of the first free kindergartens in the US.
This kindergarten was structured around the ideals of
the famous German philosopher and educator Friedrich
Froebel, whose radical educational system is considered to
have influenced the aesthetic and pedagogical foundations
of the Bauhaus. Notable artists and architects educated in
Froebel's principals include Frank Lloyd Wright, Buckmin-
ster Fuller, Wassily Kandinsky and Piet Mondrian.

Back within is a large open area, iron rails creating a
surrounding walkway—clearly part of the original ferry.
The center is filled with water, some of which laps gently
over the walkway on one side. We stare into the sunlit

green water and see a stairway down, its lower rungs disappearing in the depths.

In a room further back we find a large spiral staircase, partially collapsed, stripped down to its two-by-fours, and covered in broken glass. We go up. There are two more floors above. More rotting wood and wire, but little else. We look out from what may have been a terrace and notice our structure appears to be fused to a large rusted barge, now home to a small meadow of yellow wildflowers.

Coda

The waterfront won't leave me alone. For years I had put off finding a new studio, one where I could work without distraction. When the *Silent Beaches* show ended I began to search. There was nothing affordable that was both private and quiet. Finally, through a series of odd connections, I was given the name of a family who owns property along the water in Red Hook, Brooklyn. My new studio is right on the Harbor. It greets me with the scent of ocean mingled with diesel fuel from idling barges and buttery crust from the Key Lime Pie guy next door. In the distance container ships form a line, waiting their turn to come into port. Lady Liberty looks on silently.

"Miss Newton Creek" and Reshaping Disaster

Granville Ganter

Reflecting on Elizabeth Albert's remarkable exhibit, *Silent Beaches, Untold Stories*, documenting the history of New York City's waterways, I've been ruminating on the problem of making art out of man-made destruction. The collection is a stunning assembly of images that document the environmental consequences of New York's commercial development over the past 200 years: vagrant workers sorting trash for barges, mountains of husked oyster shells harvested from Staten Island, and the relics of abandoned factories on the poisoned waters of the Gowanus and Newtown Creeks. It is a stunning and educational glimpse into New York's history and the strange lives and grotesque deaths that occurred on its desecrated aquatic margins. The years of research that went into Albert's show have been refined to give any casual observer a haunting knowledge of New York City's industrial past.

As much as the exhibit educates us about New York City's past and chastens us about its injustices, it also attracts with a rich aesthetic power. The show—a term I

employ loosely, as if it were meant to entertain—moves me
with its choice of details, all wrought together in a stunning
artistic mosaic. This claim puts me in an uncomfortable
place: how dare I discuss beauty or art in the face of such
environmental destruction? Like a literary critic drawing
attention to Primo Levi's descriptions of shoes in *Survival
in Auschwitz*, focusing on an artistic choice which unexpectedly materializes the human tragedy and the existential
absurdity of the ways in which people's lives were taken at
the death camps, how do we begin to disentangle aesthetic
appreciation from ethical imperatives? Perhaps this line of
questioning smacks of a simple-minded approach to art, a
remnant of my own Anglo-American Puritanism, but it
has dogged me since I first saw the exhibit.

These are big questions, and perhaps best answered
in terms of the specific contexts involved. Destruction
comes in many different forms. The environmental disaster
of Newtown Creek, for example, contains a multitude of
stories, not all of which are petrochemical nightmares.
My departure point for a tentative answer is an illustration
from a different recent gallery exhibit called "Both Sides
of the Pulaski," that featured artists from both ends of the
Pulaski bridge that connects Long Island City, Queens,
on the north shore of Newtown Creek, and Greenpoint,
Brooklyn, on the south. The painting is called *"Miss Newtown Creek."* I'll start with this image because it is a forceful
illustration of making art out of the mess we live in, featured here as a somewhat amphibian telos (Image 1).

Part shark, part soldier, and part woman, "Miss Newtown" emphasizes a transformational ethos. It underscores
the changing identity of Long Island City's environment
and citizenry, and the art itself is a manifestation of that
shift. She's not a pretty pinup. On one level, the image itself

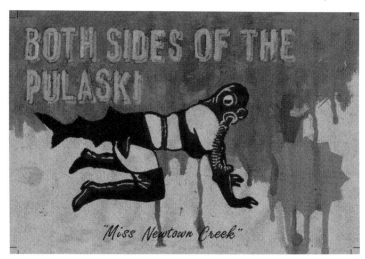

Image 1: Monte Antrim, *"Miss Newtown Creek."*

is a sad burlesque of humanity—an erotically postured fish-girl equipped to inhabit a toxic new environment— but on another level it projects a defiant resistance as well. Deformed, "Miss Newtown" is still a survivor, if not a predator. The image itself is a commentary on the kind of art that the area has produced—the art of a border world where the human and the inhuman have blended. Even her name emphasizes the act of starting over again.

"Miss Newtown" is by Monte Antrim, a Long Island City (LIC) artist who has been sketching and documenting the Greenpoint and Long Island City areas for over a decade. Like the neo-Marxist Situationists, who articulated a political and theoretical scaffold for protest art, "Miss Newtown" is both a political intervention and an attempt to take back the area on behalf of human life. Other artists have also been drawn explicitly to documenting the Newtown Creek's curious state of evolution.

Anthony Hamboussi, with whom Antrim has also collab-
orated, produced a stunning collection of photographs
taken from the roof of his van from 2002–2005. The work
of Antrim and Hamboussi has also appeared in book about
Long Island City called, *LIC: An Unorthodox Guide.*[1] The
work of these artists centers on the intersection of urban
architecture and the historical past. Depending on one's
point of view, their art might be seen as a simple critique
of industrial blight. However, from another point of view,
both artists' work has a remarkably presentist, documen-
tary feel—as if to declare, without sentimentalization or
apology, *this* is the space we inhabit. The courage of that
gaze moves away from a nostalgic lament about sad history
to engagement with more open-ended questions of documenting how we actually live in the present.

Sitting right across from 42nd St., the Newtown Creek
drains slowly into the East River—a situation that was ideal
for industrial barge traffic in the late nineteenth century.
Formerly surrounded by relatively unused swampy terrain,
the creek became a place of petroleum, chemical, and metal
manufacturing. Like many port city rivers, the Newtown
Creek was a useful means to build and ship items
via water, but it never had a large population. The Greenpoint shipyard built the Civil War ironclad known as the
Monitor, which sailed out of Newtown Creek into the East

1   Situationist International Archive, http://www.cddc.vt.edu/sionline/
si/situ.html; Anthony Hamboussi, *Newtown Creek: A Photographic
Survey of New York's Industrial Waterfront* (New York: Princeton
Architectural Press, 2010); Paul Parkhill and Katherine Gray, *LIC in
Context: An Unorthodox Guide to Long Island City*, illustrations by
Monte Antrim, photography by Anthony Hamboussi (Brooklyn, NY:
Furnace Press, 2005). For a good history of LIC, see also Vincent
Seyfried, *300 Years of Long Island City, 1630–1930*. (Garden City, NY:
V.F. Seyfried, 1984).

Image 2: Aerial view of Long Island City and Greenpoint.

river in the 1860s. Once a bustling commuter ferry departure point to midtown Manhattan, the Newtown Creek area
lost traffic when it was bypassed by the Queensborough
Bridge in the early twentieth century, and the area sank
back to being a fairly unpopulated zone of light industry.
In the later twentieth century, it became the desolate home
of lower class Irish, Polish, and Italian families. Oil storage
and chemical manufactories continued to function there,
built on landfill from New York City's street sweepings. As
Albert's *Forgotten Beaches* emphasizes, Newtown Creek is
famous for a massive oil spill and subterranean explosion
in the 1950s, still leaking today, and the area still remains
among the top federal Superfund sites designated for clean
up. This twentieth century photograph of the area (Image 2),
taken from Albert's exhibit, shows Long Island City on the
north side of the creek, and Greenpoint on the south.

Until the 1990s, when the zoning regulations finally changed to allow skyscrapers to be built, LIC was a grim borderland, plagued by constant low-level petroleum fumes seeping from the ground, and powerful gusts of pulpy-rotten air coming off the open sewage treatment plant across the creek in Greenpoint. As "Miss Newtown's" gasmask reminds us, smell has been one of the central elements of the Long Island City experience, at least over the past century. Living there in 1994, I was wakened in the night by a stench so strong that I did not know whether to open the window or shut it. Either seemed like a bad decision, so my wife and I got in the car and drove north to Astoria for a few hours. My favorite quote from the *Forgotten Beaches* exhibition is the one from the *New York Times* describing the Newtown Creek in 1887: "a quivering envelope of nauseous fog hangs above the place like the pall of death." I know what they were smelling.

Despite the scuzziness of LIC, some people liked it because it was quiet and open—there were many abandoned lots between its factory buildings, few of which were taller than three floors. I kept a canoe in the backyard to paddle up the creek on sunny days. Even now, you can park your car all year round in LIC, which doesn't have alternative side of the street parking, because there simply haven't been many people who want to live there. Since the 1990s there's been a change—large tower-shaped housing developments have been built on the water for young professionals who commute on the 7 train to Manhattan, and the area is rapidly becoming gentrified—a bedroom community for those who need rapid access to Manhattan but can't afford to live there yet.

The Newtown Creek's historically working-class population, however, is probably why they were able to build the methane harvester on the river in Greenpoint, one of the biggest in the country (Image 3). Its technical name is the Newtown Creek Wastewater Treatment Plant but locals call it the Shit Tits, or the Fart Factory. It processes sewage and can potentially capture the combustible methane gases that rise from the sewage and turn them into fuel. It is built adjacent to the sites of the old refineries that polluted the Newtown Creek in the first place.

The site is as large as an atomic reactor, and oddly, the architects and the city have turned it into a kind of tourist attraction with a visitors' center and a nature walk. Lighting artist Hervé Descottes designed its evening aspect, which is bathed in Blade Runner-ish blues (Image 4).

This gigantic testament to industrial power is a fitting sepulchre for Newtown Creek, a paradoxical acknowledgment of the sins committed by heavy industry in the area, and a peculiar advertisement for the neighborhood at the same time. As the city's promotional website about the plant declares, the wastewater plant aspires to a kind of modernist commentary—its curious shape proclaimed by its job, the digestion of waste. Its bold and unexpected shape makes me think of "Miss Newtown," a far less commercially subsidized project, but one which seems to share a similar ethos. Both works emphasize the processing of gas and outlandish utilitarian designs for survival. Both are examples of the reciprocal reshaping of a toxic environment and human culture.

One is tempted to describe the Newtown plant as a contemporary example of the industrial sublime. In the late nineteenth century, such huge buildings of boilers and

Image 3: Newtown Creek Wastewater Treatment Plant.

Image 4: Hervé Descottes, Newtown Creek
Wastewater Treatment Plant night treatment.

smokestacks signified the triumph of man's power over nature, a prideful, if not an arrogant claim of man's agency. This view is profoundly anthrocentric, however, and only a half truth.

A better way to think about the plant, and mankind's relationship to the environment more generally, not only recognizes the complimentary forces at work at a site like the Newtown Creek Wastewater Treatment Plant, but also the unexpected burdens put on the critical language we employ to analyze it. The interaction of environment and art is an emergent area of ecocritical discourse, where narrative transforms in a reciprocal relationship with what it purportedly describes. The ecocritic William Ruekert, and more recently, Angus Fletcher, have written about certain kinds of art and poetry in terms of their environmental ontologies.[2] For these critics, art about nature often comes to imitate the forces it describes. Poems become environments in themselves, bundles of stored energy in flux. For these critics, writing about the environment is not just a description of the processes in the environment—the words become a living allegory of the environment to the extent that they actually become parallel worlds. The successful work of art, the successful environmental poem, is the one that doesn't simply enthrone the anthrocentrism of the artist. Rather, the ecological work of art shows the interaction of systems, the interplay of both human and inhuman actors. The ecocritic Timothy Morton has

2   William Ruekert, "Literature and Ecology: An Experiment in Ecocriticism," *The Ecocriticism Reader*, ed. Cheryl Glotfelty (Athens: University of Georgia Press, 1990), 105–123; Angus Fletcher, *A New Theory for American Poetry: Democracy, the Environment, and the Future of Imagination* (Cambridge: Harvard UP, 2006).

described this interaction as a "mesh" of human and inhuman forces in his book *The Ecological Thought* (as well as in his YouTube videos).[3] Morton's insight is pretty easy to visualize in Ralph Waldo Emerson's well-known invocations of the sunset in *Nature* where he mutually dilates and conspires with the morning wind, or in Whitman and Dickinson's nature scenes, or in *Moby Dick*'s ocean, which insistently returns us to the world beyond Ahab's (or even Melville's) control.

To art critics, of course, the successful work of art magically conspires with the world around it, and even changes the language of criticism we use to talk about that relationship. Literary studies may initially seem like an unlikely place to derive a vocabulary for discussing the relation between art and the environment, but a host of terms allied with the concept of *metaphor* helps get at the transgressive bridge between apparently unrelated objects: *metalepsis* and *transumption*—when a figure from an older context is copied into a new one, a relation that exerts a backwards and forward force on both the original and new context; *catachresis*—frequently cited as a poetic "failure" when words are forcefully *mis*used, such as the smell of a sound, but which inspired poets often employ to tease out a new idea. These poetic terms are sometimes classed as "master tropes" by literary scholars because they capture the bold way that the arts typically break commonsense rules to emphasize new relations between people and things. Literature thrives on these unsanctioned relationships

3   Timothy Morton, *The Ecological Thought* (Cambridge: Harvard UP, 2012).

that illustrate uncomfortable connections between objects and ideas.

From this position, it's hard not to see the Newtown Creek Wastewater Treatment Plant as a titanic acknowledgement of the interaction of environmental forces, of which the human contributions play only a part. As surely as its oversized eggs emphasize human management of gas, an attempt to control nature—the architecture is a giant metalepsis or catachresis of the power of the environment itself.

I was drawn back to the exhibition several times over the autumn of 2013, because I couldn't come up with a very neat hook, and I now realize that that is what kept me coming back. I'm struck by the moral outrages depicted here, of grim border worlds where the poor are set to scavenge amidst industrial refuse either by cruel business design, governmental program, or individual enterprise, but the exhibit is much richer than a reformist polemic. Blooming from the waste are life forms. I think Albert's exhibit is itself an emblem of that process of rebirthing and rebalancing and reusing, of picking up the pieces. I'm struck also by the artists' presentations with it, like Spencer Finch's "The River That Flows both Ways," the multi-panel series of the varied colors of the Hudson River, a spectrum of the ideas the exhibition as a whole offers— from blue to green to brown, a somber illustration of the various faces of the river. The more I look at it the more I like it—it reminds me of the Hudson I know and re-shapes it for me too.

I think also of the series of local geographical portraits that Monte Antrim's "Miss Newtown" is a part of, such

Image 5: Monte Antrim, *End of Apollo*.

as his work (Image 5) called the *End of Apollo* (Street), in Greenpoint, near where the Bushwick canal once emptied into the East River, a part of forgotten history that Albert's exhibit so importantly recovers for us.[4]

Life emerges from the mess of failure, sometimes in spite of our guilt, and sometimes with our help too.

4   Monte Antrim, "End of Apollo," *Local Rides, Modern Girls, Sketchbooks* (Monte Antrim, 2012).

Arctic-Oceanic New York

Lowell Duckert

> I would that my name be carved on the tablets
> of the sea.
>
> —Letter from Henry Hudson
>   to Richard Hakluyt

> Hudson achieved in 1609 nothing memorable,
> even by this new way.
>
> —Hessel Gerritz[1]

In the summer of 1609, under orders from the
Dutch East India Company to venture north by
northeast towards the Russian archipelago of Novaya
Zemlya, the English navigator Henry Hudson erred:
thwarted by icepack, and unwilling to return so soon
to his Dutch patrons, he sailed west instead, journeying
down the North American coast that his friend John
Smith had described to him. Entering what we now
know as New York Harbor in September 1609, he sailed
up a river called the North River, a waterway that Italian
explorer Giovanni da Verrazano sighted in 1524 but never

---

1   Hudson quoted in Edward Butts, *Henry Hudson: New World
    Voyager* (Toronto: Dundurn Press, 2009), 30–1; Gerritz quoted in
    G.M. Asher's volume for the Hakluyt Society, *Henry Hudson the
    Navigator* (New York, Burt Franklin, 1860), 187.

explored. Traveling as far north as modern-day Albany
before the shallow waters forced him to turn back, Hudson's journey helped establish the city of New Amsterdam
for the Dutch, making him, arguably, the founder of
New York City and the face behind the Hudson River.
But Hudson was not looking for the isle of Manhattan or
interested in the economic potential of the river valley;
first mate Robert Juet's dull descriptions of the landscape,
printed in Samuel Purchas's *Pilgrimes* (1625), prove this
point: "The land grew very high and mountainous. The
river is full of fish....The mountaynes look as if some
metall or minerall were in them."[2] Juet's cursoriness belies
Hudson's *true* intention, however: he hoped to find the
Northwest Passage, the fabled route to Cathay the English
eagerly coveted and even—according to the magus John
Dee—*deserved* as inheritors of King Arthur's legendary
conquest of the northern ocean. This river, so Hudson
thought, would finally make his country a global (colo-
nial) power.

Thus a city that often emphasizes its ties to the Atlantic Ocean owes it inception in part to another ocean: the
Arctic. New York City is a city, we might say, that began
because of Hudson's geographical *error* upriver. I purpose-
fully use this word in its etymological sense of the Latin
errare ("to stray, err").[3] Hudson's geographical errancy
would negatively affect his image for years to come;
consider the Dutch publisher Hessel Gerrtiz's dismissive
summation in 1612, for example, or fellow passage-seeker

---

2   Asher 83, 89. All quotations from Hudson's voyages hereafter refer to
     this edition.

3   See error, *n.* in the Oxford English Dictionary online, especially sense I.1.

and compatriot Luke Foxe's slanderous estimation of his predecessor in *North-West Fox* (1635). Recalling a moment in which Hudson sent home a "Master Coolbrand" on his fourth voyage of 1610–11, Foxe held the latter to be in "every way [...] a better man than [Hudson],"[4] for Coolbrand was the one who "devised [the] course" into the vast saltwater bay in northern America (180). For these two early modern critics, navigation implies a course and an endpoint; any "error" is that which "strays" from the *correct* path or does not reach the *right* end: a teleology fit for the straight lines of ecological imperialism. Errors cost dearly to them, and it would be errors that ultimately claimed Hudson's life: he died on the fourth voyage in that body of water that now bears his name, Hudson Bay, a victim of mutiny, set adrift by his men who deviated from their captain's orders. Hudson's expressed wish to Hakluyt came true. No other name has more volume of water attached to it. But if I may offer an opinion of my own, Hudson's errancy suggests a kind of "erring" that does not demand an endpoint. To "stray" without something to stray *from*: when accidents are wished for, when erroneousness is an endless change in direction rather than missing a mark.[5] No one knows where Hudson's bones lie, yet we can imagine a bodily metamorphosis under ice, an Arctic version of Ariel's song that carves his name "on the tablets of the sea," that proves how erraticism is the stuff

---

4   Quoted in Asher, 180.

5   I liken Hudson to Michel Serres's Ulysses: "The Odyssean path is an exodus rather than a method. An exodus in the sense that the path deviates from the path and the track goes off track." *The Five Senses: A Philosophy of Mingled Bodies*, trans. Margaret Sankey and Peter Cowley (New York: Continuum, 2008), 261.

that dreams and obsession are made on, including our own.[6] "Hudson" and Hudson: errors both, *still* erring.

~~~~~~~~~~~~~~~~~~~~~~

During the last Ice Age, 1.5 million to 10,000 years ago, the Wisconsin ice sheet stretched from present-day Montana to Massachusetts. About 50,000 years ago, this mobile mass of ice entered the current New York metropolitan area, sculpting places like Long Island and speckling the landscape with till and moraines we call city parks: Inwood Hill, Wolfe's Pond, and Van Cortlandt.[7] Nowadays the river barely changes in elevation from where it begins at Lake Tear of the Clouds on the slope of Mt. Marcy in the Adirondacks, shifting only about 5 feet in its 145-mile trip to the ocean.[8] Around 13,500 years ago, however, the river was not as consistent. When "The Great Flood of New York" occurred, Iroquois Lake (now Lake Ontario) burst through its ice dam, sending a torrent of freshwater sluicing south down the glacial river valley where it emptied into the North Atlantic and initiated a global climate change. The valley still extends below water, in fact, and for this reason the Hudson is sometimes referred to as the "drowned river." The topography of New York City, in short, is

6   Corey Sandler's *Henry Hudson: Dreams and Obsession* (New York: Citadel Press, 2007) is a fitting example. See "Part V: Deciphering the Hudson Code" in particular.

7   See http://www.nycgovparks.org/about/history/geology for more information.

8   Douglas Hunter follows the river in great detail in *Half Moon: Henry Hudson and the Voyage That Redrew The Map of the New World* (New York: Bloomsbury Press, 2009).

Image 1: Glacial erratics in Central Park.

glacial. In addition to the parks abovementioned, other
Arctic remnants are more obvious (Image 1). Inner city
rocks like this one in Central Park are what geologists call
"glacial erratics," boulders deposited at sites in which they
conspicuously stand out from native rocks, straying from
their "proper" place amongst mineralogical kind, and,
perhaps in this specific case, from their rightful place in
"rural" settings. As geological erratics, they remind us of
an ice age supposedly *past*, static objects around which we
recreate ourselves in the present.

But such erroneous geomaterial, like Hudson's
de/re/composing Bay-body, forges a transhistorical
continuum; their surprising out-of-placeness acknowl-
edges them as arrivals that still arrive. Matter agentic and
mobile, rocky erratics remind us of being in a trans/cryo/
corporealism, of the Arctic touching us, of physically

being "us."[9] "Hudson" speaks less of the anthropocentrism
of bodies of water—river, strait, and bay—and more of
icewater bodies. So does a wander in Central Park. New
York City's unofficial anthem might yearn to "be a part of
it," but we are already part of the ice, not apart from it.[10] So
is my writing right now in mid-March 2014, insulated but
not separated from a "polar vortex" that began in January
and has not yet left North America. Unlike Hudson's
fluvial journey *north* into the Arctic, the air current now
shifts *south*. We do not need to go the Arctic; the chilling
cyclone comes to us, crawling out of its prescribed "circle,"
fostering fears that in a New York minute, *nothing* can or
will change.[11] Or that New York will become the "drowned
city" after the polar icecaps melt. "My little town blues /
they are melting away," as the song goes, but these icy blues
are not so welcome. Freeze or flood (or both): these images
remind us not just of past touches of ice, but forebode
future catastrophes to come. Whether we blame the errors
of industrial capitalism (if only we were not so rapacious
we could have remained harmonious with nature), or if we
maintain that denying the existence of climate change is a
grievous error (we cannot afford to make *this* one), we are
stranded like Hudson as the past becomes future, as river
and sea levels rise, as we pass through ages of eco-catastro-
phe, all victims adrift, erring.

9   The term "trans-corporeality" is Stacy Alaimo's, "in which the human
     is always intermeshed with the more-than-human world." *Bodily
     Natures: Science, Environment, and the Material Self* (Bloomington:
     Indiana University Press, 2010), 2.

10   Sorry, Ol' Blue Eyes: "Theme from *New York, New York*," famously
     sung by Frank Sinatra.

11   For example, see an article in *The New York Times* from January 6,
     2014: "Arctic Cold Blankets Midwest, Freezing Routines." http://www.
     nytimes.com/2014/01/07/us/arctic-cold-blankets-midwest-freezing-
     routines.html.

The Mahicans who once resided in the region Hudson helped colonize have another name for the Hudson River: *Muhheakantuck*, "the river that flows both ways." Reconceiving the Hudson as a north-south river marks an icy interchange—a circulating eddy of freeze and flood, past and future, Arctic and Atlantic—that may help us rise to the challenges of a cold waterworld differently. When John Playse recounted Hudson's first voyage of 1607 in search of the Northeast Passage, he included the captain's own notes. On the evening of July 11, Hudson complains, "we had the company of our troublesome neighbours, ice with fogge" (12). While noting such dangers is commonplace for travel writers of the north, calling ice a "neighbor" is not. "Neighbor" is a composite word from the Old English *nēahgebūr*, from *nēah* ("nigh, near") and *gebūr* ("inhabitant, peasant, farmer").[12] Contrary to Gerritz's disparagement, I believe Hudson helps us realize what we have forgotten: we exist *because* of our relationship to ice, by being "nigh" to the icy ocean. Arctic-Oceanic New York recognizes how proximity shapes ontology, observable in the hyphenated interchange (-) that "flows both ways," channeling Michel Serres's parasitical relationality.[13] It is through such a networked interchange that neighbors interact, co-constitute, coexist. And yet Hudson reminds us of displaced "neighbors," those absent presences who

12 See neighbour | neighbor, *n.* and *adj.* in the Oxford English Dictionary online.

13 "To play the position or to play the location is to dominate the relation. It is to have relation only with the relation itself....And that is the meaning of the prefix *para-* in the word *parasite*: it is on the side, next to, shifted; it is not on the thing, but on its relation." *The Parasite*, trans. Lawrence R. Schehr (Minneapolis: University of Minnesota Press, 2007), 38.

have been pushed out but leave their traces nonetheless: geographical erratics such as the Mahicans and Lenape he combats on his trip upriver, whose deaths gave Juet place-names like "Manna-hata" (91); geological erratics like the boulders of Central Park, stranded, victims of modernity's mutiny against ages "past." We should not remember Hudson's journey for its "nothing," but as a reminder of our everyday Arcticality, and act on its impulse to create ethical erratics for co-"inhabitant[s]," good neighbors, to follow. Remember 1609 not for being a failure but for it sponsoring other ways to be, "new ways" to go, chances to stray without reaching a destination—or even positing one.

A "new way," perhaps, into the geopolitics of our time in which "neighboring" nations in the Arctic look north, just as their forebears did, to metallically rich places like Greenland.[14] Will the receding ice lead to another Manhattan project against "troublesome" non/human neighbors like the Greenlandic Inuit and the ice sheet itself? Is there a "proper" course in this eddy of reality within we live? No: and this is precisely my point. We should all be glacial erratics when it comes to the *fantasy* of being apart from the Arctic, and especially when it comes to being a territorial/izing neighbor. The "Empire City" needs to reject its imperialistic title that depends, in Mick Smith's words, upon "the antipolitical and antiecological principle of sovereignty."[15] The rule of the human: what impropriety!

14   For instance, see an article in the *New York Times* from September 23, 2012: "A Melting Greenland Weighs Perils Against Potential." http://www.nytimes.com/2012/09/24/science/earth/melting-greenland-weighs-perils-against-potential.html

15   Mick Smith, *Against Ecological Sovereignty: Ethics, Biopolitics, and Saving the Natural World* (Minneapolis: University of Minnesota Press, 2011), xx.

And here is the cold corollary of refusing ontological sovereignty: letting go of the dream of *equilibrium* that will keep the Hudson Valley and its cities permanently warm and dry. Cary Wolfe notes how "*in* the future, we *will have been wrong.*"[16] His prophecy does not mean we should stop erring with the world, however, but rather to rethink errors differently than the failure to "get right" or to "find" the singular object of a given search. We will make mistakes; so what may we learn? The ice (the Ice Age) *is* coming at us, but for Hudson, the North River was also an invitation into another oceanic world rather than its foreclosure. Erraticism still is: ultimately, envisioning an Arctic-Oceanic New York assures us that passages do not terminate *up-* or downstream—they burgeon, they proliferate relations "troublesome" and otherwise (like English explorers, ice and fog, indigenous tribes, park strollers); they take us into collectives (like New Amsterdam and the eight current member countries of the Arctic Council);[17] they passage us into new/er ethical geopolitical realms that make room in their parliaments for icier citizens. Recasting a part of New York City's oceanic history as Arctic can redefine its future not just as inevitable catastrophe, but also of cryo-coexistence, polar possibilities, dreams as well as obsessions. Beginnings, not just ends, are *nigh*. We may be in the neighborhood of vorticular floes, but we are all Hudson's heirs as well.

16   Cary Wolfe, *Before the Law: Humans and Other Animals in a Biopolitical Frame* (Chicago: University of Chicago Press, 2013), 103.

17   Canada, Kingdom of Denmark, Finland, Iceland, Norway, Russian Federation, Sweden, and the United States of America. http://www. arctic-council.org/index.php/en/

#bottlesNbones

Jamie Skye Bianco

tales of oceanic remains

To begin, we could talk about silica, silicates. Sand and glass. Collectible. Recyclable. Except when they are not. I'll come back around this at the end.

Snake and tail.

Image 1: Tail of a Bottle Plain Eddy (November 10, 2012).

I used to make the trip to the bay every week,

This glass, collected, kept, discarded, exploded, buried at sea. Message *as* a bottle. Message *as* bones. Dead bottles and lively horse bones washing ashore at Dead Horse Bay, lapping the coast of Barren Island (not an island anymore) in the western part of New York City's Jamaica Bay.

> Barren Island, located on the south side of the site and the only upland within this part of the estuary, was formed as part of the system of barrier beaches along the south shore of Long Island. Barren Island was naturally low dunes and sandy beach, surrounded by the wide, open expanses of the Atlantic Ocean to the south, Jamaica Bay to the north, and the low-lying south shore of Long Island in the distance. Salt grasses covered the marshes while trees and shrubs grew on the dunes and uplands. By the nineteenth century, Barren Island was transformed into an interior island within Jamaica Bay due to storms and longshore currents, which extended Rockaway Beach, the barrier beach to the east, westward beyond Barren Island.

Dead Horse Bay returns the deposit on the bottles. As the surfacing site of New York City's horse rendering factories and underwater waste disposal from the 1880s through the 1930s, the waste that was once "capped" in the bay, now reclaims the land.

Image 2: Uncapped Bottle Plain (November 10, 2012).

Dead Horse Bay,

The third path feels like a run, a run to the shore. A final run made by the horses to the glue factory (and cosmetics and household chemicals and fertilizer and *recycling)*. This phantasy of mine is utterly inaccurate, a desire for the possibility of escape, of clean up. The horse corpses, *transportation* dropping dead in the streets of turn of the century Manhattan and Brooklyn, would have been loaded onto barges and drug via pulleys from the water into the factories extending into the water, such as the New York Sanitary Utilization Company, later closed down in 1919 due to local concerns about odors and beach pollution, forget the labor and what was happening in this *sanitary* process.

> Between 1850 and 1918, Barren Island was trans-
> formed into an industrial community built off the
> processing of dead animals and garbage from New
> York and Brooklyn. These industries were lured to
> Barren Island on account of its remote location,
> where offensive odors would not reach populated
> areas, and its access to deep navigable waters in
> Rockaway Inlet. The factories made use of the wet-
> lands and bays at the north or inland side of Barren
> Island for dumping their refuse.

But I digress. The three pathways that lead to the shore are products of the African Americans and European immi-grants who labored in the factories (and were trapped on the island by lack of transportation), by the Navy, which bought the area in 1942 and by the National Park Service, which took over the site from the Navy in 1972.

Image 3: Bottle Tree, after Sandy (December 14, 2012).

Hurricane Sandy stripped,

Bottle tree: the hopeful act of founding a making in waste

> A small community developed around the industries, with residences, churches, bars, and a school.

Washed up safe: the bottom line for this place, a place to change garbage into money

> At the height of the industrial development in the second decade of the twentieth century, the population of Barren Island reached approximately 1,500 people.

Bottle plain: revealed at low tide, it lacks in hope but abounds in nitrates and non-degradable "vintage trash" collected by hipsters and eBay micro-entrepreneurs

> In 1923, the island's isolation from the mainland was ended with the construction of Flatbush Avenue, which extended to the Rockaway Inlet shoreline of Barren Island.

Image 4: Safe Keeping (November 4, 2012).

and watch the evidence

And yet it is a place of composites, artifactuality spanning back to the 1880s. It has collected garbage back that far too. A fertilizer factory on the western edge of Barren Island silica-slipped into the water in 1890. Scores of fires. At least 32 documented factories existed between the 1850s and the 1930s: horsehair, tallow, grease, fertilizer, nail polish, tinctures, bottling of all kinds, and of course, glue.

> By the late 1920s as public pressure mounted against the waste factories, the population declined to 400 with only one of the factories remaining in business.

And we must remember, this precedes our plasticine petrochemical friendships. This is the age of composites, resin, India rubber, the stuff that garbage-degradation phantasies are made of and Dead Horse Bay happily returns a demonstration of the real as so many water-laden objects surging up intact from below the surface...return of the pre-petrochemocene.

Image 5: Brownie, Sand Captured (October 20, 2012).

flow in and out with the tides.

A convertible in red.
A tiger ring in red.
A glass vial.

> During the 1920s as the garbage industry on Barren Island was disappearing, commercial aviation was gaining popularity and municipalities throughout the country were constructing airports.

A Brownie camera corpse.
A horseshoe in red.

> To the south of the airport, the Barren Island community was slowly disappearing during this period. The city cleared the western part of the island in the mid-1930s for redevelopment as part of Brooklyn Marine Park, to be linked by other parks in the area by the Marine Parkway Bridge completed across Rockaway Inlet in 1937.

Image 6: PD, Motorcycle (October 20, 2012).

The number nine, or six, in red.
And glass bottles.

> The eastern end of the island remained in private
> ownership with its houses, church, and foundations
> of demolished factories.

Brown Rosex bleach bottle, label turned green (yes! a paper
label surviving at least 70 years of salt water later) sits next
to an Alice in Wonderland, *plastic*, tea cup.

> The Navy condemned the remaining private
> property on Barren Island by January 1942 and on
> February 9, 1942, took ownership of the city property
> through condemnation.

After Superstorm Sandy, the plastics from the Rockaways
mingled as if to claim the site for continuous refusal. No
easy claim laid for precious antique garbage when the
Park Service's waverunner sits on top of a pile of children's
objects that span a century. No barriers despite the islands.

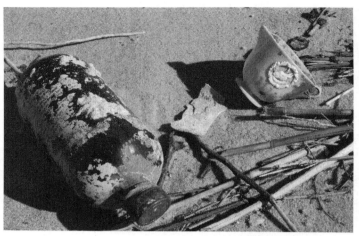

Image 7: Tea and Tincture (November 4, 2012).

The Rockaways and Breezy Point
were still in darkness.

After the storm, Dead Horse Bay became a deposition zone in testimony to the Rockaways, lit up by the ocean on the other side of that sliver of a barrier, inhabited, flooded.

> As documented on eighteenth-century maps, Barren Island was one of the barrier beaches protecting Jamaica Bay, together with Rockaway Neck (later known as Rockaway Beach or Peninsula) to the east, and another peninsula later known as Plumb Beach and Pelican Beach to the west.

One non-intuitive aspect of barriers is their mobilities.

Image 8: US Park Police, Waverunner and Boat (November 4, 2012).

Halfway through this visit,
one-third of the street lights on Breezy Point
suddenly lit up.

Strange fruit of fall: pumpkin and basketball

> As late as the mid-nineteenth century, a Brooklyn
> newspaper reported: "There is scarcely a decade
> that, through storm and wind, the configuration of
> the [Barren Island] shore and even interior divisions
> of it, is not more or less changed."

Superstorm Sandy landed late in October, 2012.

> While it is not known when Barren Island first took
> shape as a barrier island, it underwent considerable
> reconfiguration through natural forces during the
> nineteenth century. By 1839, major storms had
> joined Barren Island with Pelican Beach and Plumb
> Beach to the west, and created a new opening
> known as Plumb Inlet that separated the elongated
> barrier beach from Coney Island to the west

The *#bottlesNbones* of Dead Horse Bay land everyday. And
have for years.

> At some point between 1844 and 1898, major storms
> once again reconfigured the barrier islands, separat-
> ing Barren Island from Plumb Beach by creating a
> new inlet, identified in 1898 as Dead Horse Inlet and
> today corresponding with Gerritsen Inlet.

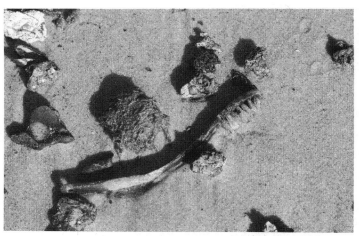

Image 9: Toothbrush, Horsehair (October 20, 2012).

We recognize suddenly
that I am filming
Dead Horse Bay.

The glamour of the catastrophic storm overwhelms the banality of an everyday, 100+ year old, continuously productive, underwater garbage heap. (Always at your constant disposal.)

> One of the most dramatic changes to the system of barrier beaches at Jamaica Bay was the elongation of Rockaway Beach toward the west. While aligned with Barren Island's barrier beach during the eighteenth century, over the next century Rockaway Beach extended into the ocean west and south beyond Barren Island, lengthening more than a mile between 1866 and 1911.

I am guilty in this. The storm and its correlate in climate change are second cousins to this strange shifting bay, sharing little and everything material with The Rockaways. Garbage for now; shifting sands for centuries.

> Although created by natural forces, this accelerated lengthening of the beach was caused in part from construction of jetties, grain fields, and other beach stabilization structures that were erected to protect beach-front communities. Aside from changing the setting of Barren Island and its ecological function as a barrier beach, the extension of Rockaway Beach also shifted Rockaway Inlet from the east to the south sides of Barren Island, causing the old ocean beach on Barren Island to be washed away.

What does bring these two together? The break in their capacities to block because of what humans throw into the water? Between 1866 and 1911, the Rockaways "grew" over a mile in westerly length. These years correlate directly with the years of industrial production on Barren Island.

Image 10: Trash Strata, Bottles and
Plastic Transportation (November 4, 2012).

But we are looking at the other world.
The Rockaways.

The urn.
The pipe.
The plastics.
The boats.
The boards.
The 78s.
The beams.

Image 11: Urn and Pipeline (November 10, 2012).

The heaps.

> Prior to the extension of Rockaway Beach in the
> early nineteenth century, the southern shore of
> Barren Island would have been a marine intertidal
> sand beach (ocean beach), characterized by rough,
> high-energy waves with high fluctuations in salinity
> and moisture, with no vegetation but abundant with
> marine life and shorebirds.

Wreckage.

> Above the high-tide level, the beach would have
> transitioned to a maritime dunes community, dom-
> inated by grasses and low shrubs, including beach
> grass, dusty miller, beach heather, bearberry, beach
> plum, poison ivy, and possibly stunted pitch pines
> or post oaks

Shifting sands.

> By the late nineteenth century, these ecosystems
> largely disappeared from Barren Island through
> erosion from currents in Rockaway Inlet, as well as
> nineteenth-century industrial development.

Shifting nitrates. Shifting petrochemicals. Shifting waste.

Image 12: Rockaway Plastics, Dead Horse Beach #2 (November 4, 2012).

Three pathways in. No escape.

This site tells many stories through sheer proximity of shifting sands and industry, but it also whispers tales of the nation, from the first airport in New York (used by the Coast Guard) to a World War II Navy base.

> With the United States' declaration of war following the attack on Pearl Harbor on December 7, 1941, the Navy began a massive expansion of Floyd Bennett Field....The most substantial change occurred on Barren Island, where the Navy demolished all remnants of the community and expanded the land out into Rockaway Inlet and Jamaica Bay for construction of two barracks areas, a seaplane base, and a wharf. To the north of the airport, the Navy filled in the remnants of the tidal estuary and developed an ammunitions-communications area with radio towers and high-explosive magazines.

Most recently, the parking lots of Floyd Bennett Field become militarized staging areas not for the Coast Guard or private aviators or the Navy, now long gone, and not even for fisherman or trash collectors, but for the National Guard and FEMA.

Image 13: Tidepool, Better Beverages (November 10, 2012).

Queer remnants.

The airstrip remains. Foundation pilings for three factories remain. Trash, old and new, remains. Hurricanes remain. *#bottlesNbones* remain.

> *The snake eats his own logical tail again.*
> *Lit up, like a glow stick or a match.*
> *Catches on the strike,*
> *fades fast*
> *as it consumes itself to persist.*

We might ask of our refusals and depositions: what degrades, if so much remains?

Image 14: Urn and Bottle (November 10, 2012).

Groundswell

Alison Kinney

> Despite the ironic style, the prospect suggested here of
> an alternative historical outcome, possible in certain
> circumstances, is a serious call to work for the future
> in defiance of all calculations of probability.
> —W. G. Sebald[1]

From the audience of Oceanic New York, I
marveled at the play of art, history, and maritime and
urban discovery, of erudition, imagination, and good-
will. "O beauty, o handsomeness, goodness!"[2] How could a
coalition of activists, architects, artists, and scholars—rocks,
grasses, and oysters—effluvia, flotsam, and concrete—not
succeed in shoring up brighter hopes for the city?

Steve replied to my frothing: "Like tides and storms,
might hopelessness be something that floods over us,
passes through, destructively and irresistibly?" Maybe, he
queried, hope wasn't where we were going, and hopeless-

1   W.G. Sebald, "Between History and Natural History: On the Literary
     Description of Total Destruction," in *Campo Santo*, trans. Anthea Bell
     (New York: Random House, 2005), 90–91.

2   Benjamin Britten, *Billy Budd*, An Opera in 2 Acts, op. 50, to a
     libretto by E.M. Forster and Eric Crozier (London: Boosey and
     Hawkes Ltd, 1951).

ness presented a threat that no unity could meet. With the
ice sheets melting, bureaucratic time now moves slower
than glacial time. Even with post-Sandy reconstruction
in progress, the city's most endangered neighborhoods
remain threatened. Perhaps we are better off jettisoning
both hope and hopelessness as inadequate, irrelevant bag-
gage. Both can be too easily co-opted into passivity: with
naïve, oblivious optimism in things fixing themselves; with
despair at the futility of acting, too late, against ecological
collapse. Maybe we can try to harness the rational calcula-
tions of the hopeless, yet choose to act *as though* we believe
we can make a difference.

"When I sit by myself...and I know that the world is
such a way, and I know that the world needs to be such
another way, am I able to live with myself and get up in the
morning and act according to what I know is true? Have I
done what needs to be done?" said Jay O'Hara, who, with
Ken Ward, blocked shipping to the Brayton Point coal plant
on May 15, 2013, with their lobster boat, *Henry David T.*[3]

In a global state of emergency, artists, scholars, and
writers doubt our power to make a difference. How do we
live with ourselves, if we are diligently meeting our dead-
lines for *Oceanic New York*, rather than gluing ourselves
to the TransCanada offices? I try out an answer: that the
choice between planetary survival and artistic work is
a false one. That the political assault on the humanities
perpetuates simplistic narratives of need and renewal that
serve the super-rich at the expense of the many. That we
can work together to preserve access to knowledge, art,

3   Wen Stephenson, "The New Climate Radicals," *The Nation,* July 17,
2013, accessed March 4, 2014, http://www.thenation.com/article/175316/
new-climate-radicals?page=0,0#.

and beauty as a human right, no less so for the people of Breezy Point and Red Hook.

I try another: that one thing I can do, as a writer, is to donate part of my word count to another perspective, one that stands as a hard, insistent, shining pearl, amidst all my floppy enthusiasms and doubts. Terri Bennett, a relief worker and journalist in Haiti after the 2013 earthquake, Occupy Sandy volunteer, and, co-founder of Respond & Rebuild,[4] which provided free pumping, gutting, mold remediation, and/or reconstruction to over 400 NYC homes. She spoke with me about the timelines of recovery:

I'm often asked if we should be instituting changes in how we develop cities and where we choose to live. I feel pretty conflicted about this question. You're asking people to leave who they are, fourth-generation families for whom the ocean is a huge part of community identity: that's where they see neighbors, walk dogs, exercise with friends. They say, "Don't you think this place we're from is beautiful?" And I do. So much of the Brooklyn and Queens waterfront is made of lower- and middle-class communities; you could secure a house and be a standing part of your community. For them, all this talk about resilience isn't new. There's always been people down there who've advocated for protection from jetties, more sand, different types of infrastructural changes along the beach. It's not like anybody didn't know what hurricanes do.

After Sandy, we saw guys in suits handing people business cards, saying, "If it gets to be too much, there's a way out." Then Bloomberg said we can buy out and develop in a more resilient way.

"Resilience" winds up being exclusionary, doing things on a more expensive, more profitable scale, instead of building housing stock for working-class families. Obviously, it's too early to see luxury hotels going up on the beach, but there are a lot of avenues between resilient development plans, and neoliberal housing policy and development.

We didn't want public health concerns like mold to make people think they had to sell their homes. Mold remediation costs about $15,000 for a moderate two-family house. Homebuying can cement a community; $15,000 can keep people or push them out, so we wanted to let them decide. We worked for one woman who was a retired truancy officer with a $22,000 pension. She'd raised seven kids in a three-bedroom bungalow. She wasn't getting any aid. There's going to be a shift in that, toward upper-class communities.

In the timeline of disaster, we've barely begun to see disaster capitalism. In the beginning, you have scammers and carpetbaggers, but they're the speculator middlemen, selling later to the biggest players, who have the capital to wait. With Biggert-Waters [Flood Insurance Reform Act of 2012], elevation will make or break whether or not people can stay in their homes. Even with what you've gotten from FEMA, insurance, or Build It Back, if you don't qualify for elevating, or if you're afraid of the way elevation will change the character of your neighborhood, what are you going to do? Until people find out what they qualify for, nobody's going to want to move, if they don't have to, in case they find out later they could get enough money to

rebuild. People are trying to stick it out, but...
in three years, they'll start bearing the brunt of
insurance, they'll be paying $20,000 or more a
year. We'll see a lot of people selling off to people
who can afford that. Also, there's a huge number
of renters who have no say in rebuilding or being
re-rented to. I don't think we've seen even half of
the displacement that we're going to see from this
storm. People putting $15,000 of building supplies
on credit cards, or all living on the top floor of a
house, or a hotel to stay in a school district, because
the city or federal money hasn't come—people are
piecing together recoveries that aren't sustainable.
That's another reason we have to talk about recovery in terms of five or more years.

When the next hurricane comes, I hope
we've started to rethink the way we do disaster
relief, the political economy of disaster relief. If
we're becoming concerned with climate change
and sea level rise and the public paying repeatedly
for vulnerable areas to rebuild, then let's also start
thinking of making the disaster relief industry
more efficient, frugal, and beneficial for everyone
involved. Sending money to grassroots organizations
with flexibility and familiarity with neighborhood
needs might be more effective than sending it to
national or international aid groups, but we need to
rethink other aspects, too. As you take a few steps
back, so many things become more problematic,
like volunteer organizations that fly in people from
all over the country, often to places where people
really need jobs. You think of volunteering as free
labor, but it requires resources: tools, travel, paper-

work, skilled supervision, training that a lot of local,
affected people already have, want, or need. You
can't use people who've never held a hammer, so a
part of your staff is dedicated to making sure that
regardless of skill, there is a rewarding volunteer
experience. It raises a lot of questions: Do you
spend forty dollars a day keeping each volunteer
safe and happy, or can those resources provide
jobs for people interested in construction training?
Something like 35% of the people in the Rockaways
aged 18–25 are unemployed. Don't get me wrong.
Volunteers were extremely important in Sandy
recovery. They filled a huge void left by city and aid
agencies, a lot of them became essential to our work
and to work going on in the city, and many counted
among the most amazing people I've ever met. But
we stopped running volunteer crews, because it
was never our intention to prioritize a volunteer
experience over the actual material needs of the
community, and the math stopped adding up. Then
we started helping a construction cooperative get
off the ground instead, and getting the affected
people good, paid jobs. At some point we need to
rethink the landscape of volunteer relief. In the
early stages of a disaster, it makes sense to have
as many hands on deck as possible, and there is
a lot of "unskilled" labor that is needed to begin
the process of recovery. But at a certain point, a
shift from volunteerism to forward-thinking, liveli-
hood-oriented practice was beneficial and necessary,
because we want an equitable recovery and a more
equitable future.

Also, a lot of money for reconstruction is just hitting the ground now. The aid is more organized. Which is good and bad, because the organizations that are left are less grassroots, bigger operations, more middlemen taking a cut. When you see people in shock on the streets in the first days after a disaster, it's really difficult to discuss what needs to change. But now that we have some distance, we have to discuss how to change disaster relief itself, not just disaster mitigation—a rock jetty or raising your home—but, what's the relationship between aid organizations and the city? Who are they accountable to? What's the role of the mayor's office? Why are there ten or more organizations between the federal government's billion-dollar cash roll and the residents who need a few thousand dollars to rebuild? There could be more thinking about how to make money, public and private, have the most lasting impact for the most people, and less of a feeding frenzy in which every organization, every contractor wants a part of the spoils.

The preexisting organizations who actually know the neighborhoods are the best poised from the ability and knowledge standpoint, but are also least poised to get grants and other aid, because they haven't done disaster work before and they don't have visibility beyond the scale of their neighborhoods. Community-based organizations and after-school programs didn't get the money, even though they floated huge parts of recovery. Keeping recovery money in communities should be more of a priority, at the beginning, when programs are being designed, particularly in places with enormous wealth disparities.

Robert Moses saw it as the solution to develop low-income housing on the outskirts, on the shores. Will the new wave be, "Why are we wasting all this oceanfront property on people who can't pay for it? It doesn't make sense to have low-resources people on the shores, because then it's up to the government to rebuild when there's a disaster"? The money exists, it's flowing past the same people who were on the margins even before the storm, into the hands of contractors, consultants, middlemen, nonprofits from all over the country, and government bureaucracies. Our ultimate goal is to situate people where they get to make decisions on their own, not being forced out by lack of money or fear for survival…

No one has individually pulled off the idea of resilience.

Terri's work is local and her outlook enormous; her perspective—a manifesto, a reproach, a call for practical resistance—deserves to stand on its own terms, and to be engaged with. It belongs amidst the groundswell of unlikely coalitions trying to occupy the shores, claiming them not from the ocean, but from those who would crush dissent, inspiration, and community. What a writer can do is steal space in other people's books to highlight those efforts.

City in the Sea

Bailey Robertson

> Putting something called Nature on a pedestal and
> admiring it from afar does for the environment
> what patriarchy does for the figure of Woman. It is
> a paradoxical act of sadistic admiration.
>
> —Timothy Morton, *Ecology without Nature*

"Life's a Beach"

I was born and raised in Long Beach, New York,
whose motto in Latin, "Civitas ad Mare," means "City by
the Sea." More commonly printed on tee-shirts, coffee
cups, and door mats, however, is a kind of second unofficial motto: "*Life's a Beach*." While I realize this phrase is not
particular to the trinkets of my hometown's novelty shops,
I have begun to wonder about the appropriateness of these
words to certain aspects of life here, considering the recent
history of Long Beach. Two consecutive years, 2011 and
2012, our shores, as well as those of nearby beaches, were
battered by hurricanes Irene and Sandy. "Life's a Beach"
seems to be adapting new possibilities for interpretation,
as storm events become more frequent and severe.

Previously, I believe "Life's a Beach" as a phrase made only a grand analogy available: life, like a beach, is a meandering path, with changing tides and tumults, and unknowable secrets and depths. The intended effect mirrors the Romantic Sublime. This beach that is our life supposedly is, as Timothy Morton speculates about nature in literature, set upon a pedestal. It is not only a paradise that surrounds us, but a fetishized and "Other" object onto which we project our fantasies and desires. This is the beach of postcards—beautiful, stable, a human foothold at the edge of the unknown.

In the wake of the recent storm events, I imagine a different, more frightening and urgent meaning to the phrase "Life's a Beach"—a literal one. Life, for the members of our community, is actually inseparable from the beach. After all, the land mass that is Long Beach *is* a barrier beach, on sea level, with sandy soil, despite how concrete slabs and real estate profiteers have been conspiring to turn the strip of land into a "real" city since the early 1900s. The aestheticized, Romantic implications of the coffee-cup version of the phrase would seem to be directly opposed to its literal implications. It is dangerous for there not to be boundaries between where the beach ends and our lives begin. This danger was never clearer than in the weeks that followed Hurricane Sandy. The enraged salt water rampaged over the dunes and tore the boardwalk from its foundations, breaking the windows of condos, and drowning sport utility vehicles, as the ocean met the bay in the middle of town. Those residents who had chosen to stay out the storm were shaken from their sleep to a helpless situation. They would be stranded in flood water for several days. A mix of salt water, sand, sewage, and debris gushed into the living rooms and kitchens of Long Beach homes. Many lost all they owned. The "sadistic" element of the fantasy becomes an act of masochism in the real world; we persist in this life that is harmful to us, and to the Other. If life is *really* beach, then we may find that we are a city *in* the sea, and this is not a life that we can live with.

A Celebration of the Apocalypse

The new local attitude toward living on the beach post-Sandy challenges what Morton considers a progressive ecological thought. In Long Beach the atmosphere is festive, the pledge to "Rebuild the Beach" having renewed the community's will to celebrate our lives in this place, loved equally by transplants and natives. Everyone is half-consciously celebrating the end of life as we know it. Two years after Hurricane Sandy, the majority of Long Beach citizens have rededicated themselves to the city, and are more in love than ever with the beach-faring lifestyle. Tourism seems to be at an all-time high, and new restaurants and other kinds of businesses are springing up all the time; there's even an ocean-side trapeze situated right next to a sandy barefoot mini-golf course. The bars and nightclubs are busier than ever, and the redesigned boardwalk attracts tens of thousands of visitors on weekend days. Some people are already beginning to forget how quickly everything we build can be lost.

The recovery of Long Beach may be an uplifting example of a city's ability to survive a disaster through collaboration and positivity, but it is also an indication of a deluded outlook on the reality coastal cities are facing. Another storm event would devastate this city totally, and such an event is far from impossible. "Rebuild the Beach" is part of the same elaborate fantasy as "Life's a Beach."

We imagine that if we rebuild our boundaries and our shelters, we can keep nature within proscribed limits. When we use gimmicks like trapezes and other wild diversions to reinforce these limits, we are perpetuating our fantasy in a dangerous reality. The boardwalk, forming a literal line between the beach and the rest of the city, was one of the first things to be destroyed in Hurricane Sandy and one of the first things to be rebuilt in the wake of the storm. During the construction of the original boardwalk in 1914, real estate developer William Reynolds had boards carried through town on the backs of elephants borrowed from Coney Island's Dreamland, to draw the public eye toward the project, and to evoke the wonderment and joy of the circus. The precedent for the charade of seaside development came early, and it comes as no surprise that it was always necessary to bolster the fantasy that humans are meant to lead happy and festive lives on a tiny streak of sand in the ocean. Even more impressive is the consensus implied by our living here, that we believe God and nature and the Animal Kingdom approve of our settlement. Ownership of this place has always been contested by the ocean, whose claim runs much deeper than ours does. We cannot think ecologically without accepting this ecological reality.

A Requiem for the Fantasy

I reach a certain point in my disavowal of the "Life's a Beach" fantasy where I hit a hard wall, both discursively and sentimentally. I want to insist that there is something to mourn in the loss of a fantasized relationship to the ocean. Certainly, the literary canon, and countless elements of world culture that have grown out of the ocean-fantasy, seem to plead the case for sustaining it. What seems

unaccountably missing from Morton's apocalyptic ecology
is an explanation of where our fantasy might overflow if
it is displaced from the ocean. Do centuries of mermaids
and leviathans and Sea Gods simply vanish? The icons
that are hard-wired into our way of imagining the sea have
cultural meanings that resonate beyond corporeal reality;
"the mesh" of which we are a part cannot consist only
of biological matter. In Long Beach, and elsewhere, the
imagined associations we make with the ocean, while they
may exist outside of a pragmatic ecology, are what really
allow us to experience enmeshment. An imaginative and
curious response to the ocean is what motivates its exploration, and forges the human path into a "darker" ecology.
Attempting to conceptualize nature as something that is
alien or "strange" to our minds is quite impossible. For
better or worse, against the grain of Morton's prescriptions
for ecology, future storm and flood events will probably
only promote a more enthusiastic attempt to preserve
human bonds to the seashore, and the most feasible (if
not the most progressive) ecology is one that will embrace
this tendency, rather than try to overhaul it. What we
may be left with, rather than a dark ecology, is an absurd
ecology—but better this than an ecology of drab alienation
that would lay waste to a cultural tradition, permitting only
anxiety to exist in its place.

Insensate Oysters and Our Nonconsensual Existence

Karl Steel

> But the life of a man is of no greater importance to the universe than that of an oyster.
> —David Hume, "On Suicide"

> What is prematurely, or belatedly, called the 'I' is, at the outset, enthralled.
> —Judith Butler, *Precarious Life*[1]

The earliest version of this paper, delivered at the Oceanic New York symposium, tried to change the way people normally write about oysters. Oyster books love to talk about pearls and Chesapeake Bay's oyster war; they love how oyster middens chart the passage not of cavemen but of "covemen," who followed the beds of oysters around coasts in a kind of gustatory cartography.[2] These same writers happily accept the oyster's fleshy invitation to aphrodisiacal excess. And when they look to

1   David Hume, *Dialogues Concerning Natural Religion, the Posthumous Essays, Of the Immortality of the Soul, and Of Suicide, from An Enquiry Concerning Human Understanding of Miracles*, ed. Richard H. Popkin. 2nd ed. (Indianapolis: Hackett Pub., 1998), 100; Judith Butler, *Precarious Life: The Powers of Mourning and Violence* (London: Verso, 2004), 45.

2   For a superior discussion of human development and the waters, see John R. Gillis, *The Human Shore: Seacoasts in History* (Chicago: University of Chicago Press, 2012).

New York City, they love to mourn the loss of its oyster beds, closed by pollution and over-harvesting, perhaps for good, in 1927, once home to trillions of the creatures, a seedbed for nostalgia for the grittier appetites of New York's presumably populist past.[3] I asked us to remember the oyster itself by remembering its shell, calcium carbonate, particularly important now to offset the increasing acidification of the oceans; likewise, I asked that we appreciate how prodigiously a living oyster filters water. What they ingest and don't eat, oysters eject as pseudofeces, which, coated in mucous, fall to the ocean floor to be processed by anoxic bacteria. The cleaner, deacidified water oysters leave behind is what just about everything else needs to live. I wanted us to look to projects to use bring oysters back to New York, like the architect Kate Orff's call for "oystertecture," an "invertebrate architecture" to help abate the force of hurricanes, to keep New York City safe from our future's inevitable Sandies.[4]

3   For a sampling of oyster books, see Mark Kurlansky, *The Big Oyster: History on the Half Shell* (New York: Ballantine Books, 2006); Rebecca Stott, *Oyster* (London: Reaktion, 2004); Drew Smith, *Oyster: A World History* (Stroud: History Press, 2010); Robb Walsh, *Sex, Death & Oysters: A Half-Shell Lover's World Tour* (Berkeley: Counterpoint, 2009); John R. Wennersten, *The Oyster Wars of Chesapeake Bay* (Centreville, MD: Tidewater Publishers, 1981). The libretto of an 1880 comic opera on the Chesapeake Bay Oyster Wars ("Driven from the Seas: or, The Pirate Dredger's Doom") is available online at https://digitalarchive.wm.edu/handle/10288/17235

4   For oyster facts, see the following *New York Times* articles: Andrew C. Revkin, "Students Press the Case for Oysters as New York's Surge Protector," Nov 12, 2012, sec. Opinion; Alan Feuer, "Protecting the City, Before Next Time," Nov 3, 2013, sec. NY/Region; and Douglas Quenqua, "Oyster Shells Are an Antacid to the Oceans," May 20, 2013, sec. Science. See also Kate Orff's "Oyster-Tecture" exhibit at MoMA's 'Rising Currents' 2010 Exhibition, http://www.scapestudio.com/projects/oyster-tecture/. I thank Alison Kinney for the phrase "invertebrate architecture."

And that's all of course still important, but that approach still thinks of the oyster primarily there to be used, not as food this time, but as the ocean's purifier and our salvation. The oyster in itself still remains on the outside of our care, distinct from us, exiled to where even Peter Singer left them, with the plants and the rocks, when he notoriously declared that the line between ethically significant and ethically insignificant animals lies "somewhere between a shrimp and an oyster." When Singer himself says that there's "no good reason for avoiding eating sustainably produced oysters," because oysters are no more likely to feel pain than plants do, it seems that no one could possibly remain to care about the oyster as such.[5] This helplessness, this absolute passivity of the oyster's flesh, will be the unwitting subject of this essay. I see the oyster's passivity and exposure to being injured as not as alien to our human condition, but—maybe predictably—as emblematic of it, countering both the certainty that the chief feature of humans is our agency and that oysters, being just objects, are completely outside the possibilities of justice.

This carelessness about oysters is a rare instance where the thoughts of Peter Singer and his arch-nemesis overlap. Descartes' November 1646 letter to Margaret Cavendish, Duchess of Newcastle, argues that if one believed that animals had thought, like us, and therefore an immortal soul, then one would have to believe this of all animals, oysters or sponges included, which are "too imperfect for this to credible [nimis imperfecta sunt,

5   For Singer's oyster opinions, see Peter Singer, *Animal Liberation: A New Ethics for Our Treatment of Animals* (New York: New York Review, 1975), 188; and Christopher Cox, "Consider the Oyster," *Slate Magazine*, http://www.slate.com/articles/life/food/2010/04/consider_the_oyster.html (accessed May 22, 2014).

quam ut hoc de iis judicari queat]."⁶ In other words, says
Descartes, because oysters are so evidently irrational,
animals of whatever type are basically mechanical in their
actions, like clocks. The monstrous implications and results
of this conclusion are all too easy to trace. While Descartes'
lesson would obviously outrage Singer, both still finally
write off the oyster. For both, the oyster, so helpless and so
silent, is the point where we get to stop caring.

Our effort to save animals from Cartesianism and
even Singerism might begin by giving oysters a voice. Two
examples of this rare literary trick follow, one from the
tenth century, the other from the fifteenth; readers are
invited to continue this work into their own favored oyster
literature, perhaps starting with the silent, misunderstood,
and helpless victims in Lewis Carroll's "The Walrus and
the Carpenter." The first of my examples, an Anglo-Saxon
riddle, imagines an oyster, "unable to move" (literally,
"feþelease," footless), whose first-person complaint helplessly anticipates the bestial voraciousness of some man
who will tear it open "to devour [freten] my flesh" raw.
Then, in the 1540s, we find another talking oyster, in
Giovanni Gelli's adaptation and expansion of Plutarch's
*Gryllus.*⁷ Plutarch features Ulysses's philosophical argument

6   "To the Marquess of Newcastle," *The Philosophical Writings of
     Descartes, Vol. III: The Correspondence,* trans. Robert Stoothoff (New
     York: Cambridge University Press, 1991), 304; for the Latin original in
     a version easily accessed online, see Renati Descartes, *Epistolae, Pars
     Prima* (Amsterdam: Blaviana, 1682), 109.

7   For the riddle, I use the edition and translation, with some
     modifications, from Mercedes Salvador, "The Oyster and the Crab:
     A Riddle Duo (nos. 77 and 78) in the Exeter Book," *Modern Philology*
     101.3 (2004): 400–419; for Gelli, I use Giovanni Battista Gelli, *Circe:
     Consisting of Ten Dialogues between Ulysses and Several Men*

with one of his men, since transformed by the sorceress Circe into a pig (Gryllus means "Grunter"), in which they debate the respective advantages of humanity and porcinity. The pig wins. Gelli outdoes Plutarch by letting Ulysses be out-argued by a series of increasingly complex animals until he, at last, convinces a philosophical elephant, and only the elephant, to let itself become human again. The first, and lowest, animal is, of course, an oyster, a former fishmonger, which argues that nature evidently loves oysters best, since, by outfitting them with their own home and clothes, she frees them from having to work.

Both the riddle and the philosophical dialogue grant oysters a voice through what Jane Bennett called the "touch of anthropomorphism."[8] However, while Bennett concentrates on the usually unconsidered agency of garbage heaps, earthworms, or power grids, these two oyster works speak not of agency but rather of what the oysters cannot avoid. As in "The Walrus and the Carpenter," the voice of the oyster is mainly a voice of vulnerability. These unmuted oysters say that they, like us, want to live. They want not to be injured. The oyster of the Anglo-Saxon talks about nothing but its utter helplessness, while Gelli's oyster agrees to speak only if "those confounded crabs shall not throw a stone between my two shells…[to] make a meal of me."[9]

Transformed into Beasts, Satirically Representing the Various Passions of Mankind and the Many Infelicities of Human Life, trans. Thomas Brown, ed. Robert Martin Adams (Ithaca, NY: Cornell University Press, 1963).

8   Jane Bennett. *Vibrant Matter: A Political Ecology of Things* (Durham: Duke University Press, 2010), 99.

9   Gelli, *Circe* 12.

We ought to seek out fictional experiments like these. It's good for our imagination and maybe good for our ethics and maybe even good for oysters. When we read or teach texts like these, we advance the new materialist discovery of agency in places where most people would never expect to find it. It may be exciting, even chilling, to suspend our disbelief to work out how even the most inert of animals might themselves resist, fight back, or make something new. Or call out to us. But the danger of doing this through texts like the riddle and the Gelli is that of thinking the main way to make an oyster, for example, ethically relevant is to throw our voices into it. Another danger may be exactly that "touch of anthropomorphism" in the new materialisms, which is normally a discovery that nonhuman things can, like us, act agentially. This presumes too much about what it means to be subjected to this human condition. As I will argue below, most of our existence is nonconsensual. Therefore, I am proposing that a more thorough posthumanism might work harder to move in the other direction, by concentrating not on agency but on helplessness. I plead guilty to the charge that new materialism posthumanism mystifies the relationship of humans and objects; but it's not that I want to make the table dance, but that I want to concentrate on the obtuse-ness of objects, humans and otherwise, because "agency" is only one, small way in which we all get to engage with our environment.

I will do this by taking advantage of oysters' most salient characteristic, which is not their voice, not their anxiety, nor their sensitivity, but rather the absence of any of this. As even Peter Singer reminds us, oysters are some of the most insensitive and helpless of animals. For the speaking oysters of the riddle and the dialogue, what is most notable is not their (temporary) rationality but rather their particular helplessness, their ineluctable condition of injurability, which, more than any animal, exemplifies what Derrida called the "nonpower at the heart of power."[10] What may be needed, then, is not a "touch of anthropomorphism" to bring oysters over to us but rather a "touch of oystermorphism" to recognize how much of our existence we share with theirs. If we think with oysters, or even as oysters, we might recognize how much of our life is helpless, and how small a part rationality and agency play even in our lives. This essay will finally argue that we are more like oysters than not.

We will therefore leave behind the speaking oysters of the Exeter Riddles and Gelli to get more deeply into the ancient oyster tradition in which Descartes was writing. At least since Pliny, oysters were thought primarily as the animal without motion, without family, and with virtually no capacity to react. In the later fourteenth century, John Trevisa explains that:

> The parts of the great world are so ordered and set that the highest point of the lower creature touches the lowest point of the next creature, as oysters and shellfish, which are the lowest in animal kind, surpassing but little the highest form of life of trees and plants, for oysters cannot move except in the way that kelp of the sea wags with the water, as otherwise they cling to the earth and cannot see nor

10 Jacques Derrida, *The Animal That Therefore I Am*, trans. David Wills, ed. Marie-Louise Mallet (New York: Fordham University Press, 2008), 28.

hear nor taste nor smell; but they feel only when they are touched.[11]

Philippe de Thaon's *Bestiare* (after 1121) believes that oysters are a kind of stone, which open to receive Heaven's dew "as if they were living creatures," which, having received the dew, "become again without shapes" [puis se revugnent senz faitures]."[12]

Like rocks or plants, they were insensitive to pain, with only the barest glimmer of life. This semi-lifelessness meant they were fair game for Christians, even during fast days. Fish were allowed, primarily because their flesh, being so unlike ours, was unlikely to stir up our strength and our pleasure, and because fish were creatures that are, per Aquinas, "merely bodies having in them something of a soul" as compared to "land animals," which are "living souls with bodies subject to them."[13] At least for those medievals who knew their natural history, oysters were anything but an aphrodisiac; being only barely alive, oysters were perfectly suited—according to one

11   John Trevisa, trans. *Polychronicon*, ed. Churchill Babington, Vol. II (London: Longmans, Green, and Co., 1869), 181, "Also as it is in þe parties of þe grete world þat þey beeþ so i-ordeyned and i-sette þat þe ouermese of þe neþer kynde touche þe neþermeste of þe ouer kynde, as oistres and schelle fishe, þat beeþ as it were lowest in bestene kynde, passeþ but litel þe perfeccioun of lyf of treen and of herbes, for þey mowe not meue hem but as culpes of þe see waggeþ wiþ þe water, elles þey cleueþ to þe erthe and mowe noþer see ne hire, ne taste, ne smelle, but onliche fele when þey beeþ i-touched."

12   In Thomas Wright, ed. and trans. *Popular Treatises on Science Written During the Middle Ages* (London: Y.R. and J.E. Taylor, 1841), 127.

13   For the Aquinas, see his *Summa Theologica* I.72, "On the Work of the Sixth Day," and II.II.147, Art. 8, "The meats from which it is necessary to abstain."

fifteenth-century civic record—to signify the "sadnesse and abstinence of merth [that] shulde followe...an holy tyme."[14]

In all these writers, oysters function mainly to occupy or delineate the space between inside and outside, in this case, between life and nonlife, animal and plant, and pain and a kind of mostly invulnerable life. Or they function to imagine the helpless materiality of fleshly life, animal life at its most stonelike.[15] They do this in two ways: the first, as materializing life in its foundational quality, where on the scale of existence stones come to life, so here, then, is the bare basis for material animal life; and second, oysters materialize life in its insensible, material exposure to harm, to need, and to simply needing to be here or anywhere at all.

The oyster's animal existence could not register more faintly on our attention, just as our own basic fleshy existence does not tend to register on ours, until, of course, something goes wrong. For all that, the oyster exists, plant- and rocklike as it is. And as such, the oyster is vulnerable. This inescapable condition is what ties us to oysters most strongly, for whatever the considerable uses of reason and speech, neither can eliminate our fundamental vulnerability.

We're now in a position to reconsider Descartes' letter to Cavendish. This short letter only slowly gets to its conclusive denial of thought and soul to nonhuman

14 The quotation is from one account of the Lenten costume John Gladman supposedly wore for his January 25, 1443, revolt in Norwich; cited from Chris Humphrey, *The Politics of Carnival: Festive Misrule in Medieval England* (Manchester, UK: Manchester University Press, 2001), 66.

15 For an exhilarating stirring up of stone, now see Jeffrey Jerome Cohen, *Stone: An Ecology of the Inhuman* (Minneapolis: University of Minnesota Press, 2015).

animals, and this it does only by retreating to faith: Descartes just insists that it would be absurd to believe that oysters, and so on, would have immortal souls. This is itself a kind of mechanical reflex, a rare instance where Descartes' free thought snaps neatly into place because of instinct. The irony starts earlier though, as much of the letter is instead about the automatism of most human life. It explains that somnambulant humans sometimes swim across rivers they could never cross while awake; for the most part, we need not think in order to be able to eat or walk; and if tried *not* to cover our face as we fell, we would fail. Our fellow humans may themselves be driven only mechanically, even in their most apparently thoughtful moments. All Descartes can say confidently is that, unlike animals, we ourselves can communicate things not relating to our passions, but, at least in this letter, he provides no sustained proof that the communication even of other humans is anything but mechanical repetition. That is, only irrational custom or an equally irrational sympathetic guesswork protects Descartes' human fellows from being eaten, used, and vivisected. This guesswork overlays a more fundamental animal condition that is, for the most part, unconscious. Like other animals, we have our passions; like other animals, our passions have us, and our expressions— of hunger, of self-protection, of motion—are the voice not of our freedom but of our vulnerable bodily existence. To use Descartes' image, we may not be clocks, not entirely, but we are *mostly* clocks.

For even Descartes begins by admitting that the dominant condition of being human is unwilled exposure. Our existence is at its root not chosen, not rational, not elective, but rather, primarily, nonconsensual. We flatter ourselves by thinking that our freedom of choice is our defining characteristic, but we might ask, with Derrida, "whether what calls itself human has the right rigorously to attribute to man…what he refuses the animal."[16] We do not chose to be born. We do not chose the conditions of our being here any more than an oyster does. Our much vaunted ability to willingly move, which we hold out over the oysters, still doesn't untether us from having to live *somewhere.* The same goes for our ability to seek out our food rather than just receive it as the water gives it, like an oyster, because we still must eat. Whatever the powers of our agency to supplement our fundamental inadequacy by building ourselves homes, by wrapping ourselves in clothes and armor, we can never eliminate our vulnerability. We cover ourselves for the same reasons, and with the same necessity, that oysters do.

We can now reconsider and even reverse the standard hierarchy of being that holds humans superior to plants and plants superior to rocks. The tradition is neatly expressed by the fifteenth-century Middle English *Mirror of St Edmund*:

> You may see God's wisdom if you attend to what kind of being God to each creature. Some he has given to be only, without anything more, like stones. To others, to be and to live, like grass and trees. To others, to be, to live, and to feel, like beasts. To others, to be, to live, to feel, and to judge rationally, like men and angels.[17]

16 Derrida, *Animal that Therefore*, 135.

17 In *Religious Pieces in Prose and Verse*, ed. G.G. Perry. 1867. EETS o.s. 26. 2ⁿᵈ ed. (London: Kegan Paul, Trench, Trübner, 1913), 22, "His wysdom may þou see if þou take kepe how he [God] hase gyffen to ylke a creature to be. Some he hase gyffen to be anely, with-owtten mare, als vn-to stanes. Till oþer to be & to lyffe, als to grysse and trees.

Usually, in Descartes for example, the last, rational kind of
being is thought to be the most important. With reason,
or so the story goes, we can do nearly anything. Through
it, we can separate ourselves from our immediate circum-
stances and from every other living thing and then finally,
at least in mainstream medieval Christianity, we might live
forever through our immortal rational soul rejoined with
a perfected body, so escaping vulnerability altogether. But
among created things, only angels escape being tethered to
the previous kinds of being. For everything else, every kind
of being is additive, supplementing rather than replacing
the previous ones. We could therefore read this hierarchy
of being as one in which the final rational addition is a
veneer over an existence that is mostly animal-like, plant-
like, or stonelike. Like angels, humans can reason, but they
also have the same capacities—and accompanying vulnerabilities and needs—as beasts, plants, and rocks.

In this time of climate change, a time, perhaps
more than any other, in which the greatest forces are not
bounded individuals but rather hyperobjects, far beyond
our understanding, we should remember ourselves as
being as helplessly and perhaps as ignorantly enthralled
to the dangers as any oyster.[18] As Judith Butler observes

Till oþer to be, to lyffe, to fele, als to bestes. Till oþer to be, to lyffe, to
fele, and with resone to deme, als to mane and to angells. For stanes
erre, bot þay ne hafe nogte lyffe, ne felys noghte, ne demes noghte.
Trees are; þay lyffe, bot thay fele noghte. Men are; þay lyffe, þay fele,
and þay deme, and þay erre with stanes, [þay] lyffe with trees, þay fele
with bestes, and demys with angels."

18   See Timothy Morton, *Hyperobjects: Philosophy and Ecology after
the End of the World* (Minneapolis: University of Minnesota Press,
2013); see also Steve Mentz's post-equilibrium ecology, expressed, for
example, in "Strange Weather in King Lear." *Shakespeare* 6.2 (2010):
139–152.

in *Precarious Life* and *Frames of War,* most of us are compelled to be more exposed than others, most of us unheard, and most made more helpless than others; some of us like to pretend we are exempt, but ultimately, we are all vulnerable. All of us are more or less wittingly in a risk society, and even if we assemble the kinds of amateur scientific knowledge Stacy Alaimo traces in her *Bodily Natures* to learn just what in this environment is poisoning us, we still might find ourselves only more aware of our helpless enthrallment, without having solved the problem of just having to be here.[19] All we might come to know is what the oyster of the Anglo-Saxon Riddle already knows, that something, completely insensitive to us, is coming to devour us and to move on, without knowing.

19   Stacy Alaimo, *Bodily Natures: Science, Environment, and the Material Self* (Bloomington: Indiana University Press, 2010).

Super Ocean 64

Matt Zazzarino

I

Once, when my family was still living in Queens and I was still counting my age with the fingers on one hand, an older cousin gave me a stack of unwanted Sega Genesis games at a Christmas Eve party. Ten or twelve games total, but the only one that mattered was the boxless promotional copy of *Sonic the Hedgehog* at the top of the pile. At the time, I couldn't get enough of Sonic, Sega's "edgy" new mascot, their answer to Nintendo's Mario—I read the monthly comic books, I watched both animated series, I had coloring books and pajamas and action figures, and of course, I played the video games. But there were other kids at the party that night whose parents were depending on the Sega to keep occupied, and although I didn't understand how anyone could tire of watching me ace zone after zone of *Sonic*, majority rule won out and we started making our way through the other games I'd been given: *Ninja Turtles* was fun, but repetitive; none of us could navigate the playbook in *Madden 94*; making sense of *Toejam & Earl* required access to certain psychotropic drugs, the existence of which we were still too innocent to know.

Soon we came to a game called *Ecco the Dolphin*.

This game was weird. The eponymous hero was hardly stylized at all, as close to photorealism as the technology then allowed. Ecco was a "real" dolphin, and as far as we could tell, he seemed totally powerless in the face of all his presumed enemies. Sharks and barracudas came careening into Ecco from every direction and no button on the controller—not A, not B, not C—seemed to have any effect on anything. You were even required to come up for air every so often, or the dolphin would drown.

We were baffled. Not because we didn't understand the biological needs of sea-dwelling mammals, but because this utter vulnerability defied video game logic. What were Ecco's superpowers, and why wasn't he using them to turn enemies into points? Maybe I couldn't have articulated it then, but my deep discomfort with Ecco must have stemmed from the unconscious sense that he was, in effect, the anti-Sonic.

For those who don't know, Sonic is a cobalt blue, anthropomorphic hedgehog with the ability to run faster than the speed of sound—i.e. at *supersonic* speeds—and playing a Sonic game well is all about maintaining continuous high-speed movement via well-timed jumps and rolls. As long as Sonic is moving fast enough, when he meets a body of water he will run right over its surface, unhindered and unfazed by the momentary shift in topography. In this light, Ecco already seemed to have failed the game—he was down beneath the surface of the water from the start, he was subject to the very forces video game heroes were supposed to flout.

And so we spent what felt like hours exploring the first level, this post–Game Over purgatory, none of us with a clue what to do, fearing we were stuck in some kind of hellish Sisyphian torture game—or God forbid, a *simulator*—until someone managed to find a path forward, a tunnel in the deep.

The other kids and I swam our little dolphin farther into the tunnel, while units of oxygen disappeared from the meter at the top of the screen. After a moment, a number of killer whales torpedoed past Ecco, fleeing some invisible off-screen threat up ahead. I wonder though, if this panicked pod of orcas really felt so ominous then, or if it seemed only another pretty set-piece, another boring exhibit at the iQuarium, because in the end we paid the whales no real mind and charged ahead onto the next screen, hoping that the Video Game Stuff was about to begin.

None of us was ready for the creature lying in wait.

II

This octopus—The Octopus—deserves the Lovecraft treatment, to be rendered in terrifying and elaborate detail, endowed with a cosmic evil beyond the scope of any human comprehension. It deserves to debut after an unnerving two-hour introduction shot by John Carpenter, not ten-to-fifteen minutes of disinterested digital tourism. Instead I must improvise, approximate, and say that we saw a flash the color of an unripe orange dominate the display, saw rapacious tentacles stretch toward Ecco, saw a single bulging black eye staring back at us from the other side of the screen. What did Nietzsche say about the abyss? I shot up from the couch, ripped the cartridge out of the console, turned the TV off.

The vast majority of people figure out pretty early in life that it's borderline impossible to describe a nightmare to someone else without coming off silly. (The few who don't become insufferable social pariahs, or writers.) In all likelihood, my abbreviated description of the Octopus has only reinforced this point. But I want to make it clear that I don't invoke nightmares here for the sake of simile alone. For years after this first meeting of ours, I continued to dream horrifying dreams of the Octopus on a very regular basis. Not long after the original incident, once my family had left Queens and relocated to the Hudson Valley, nightmares of the Octopus forced me to chicken out on my first sleepover at a friend's house. I woke up convinced the blanket his mother had laid out for me was a roiling sea, that the kraken was just beneath me, preparing to suck me under. I cried and cried until my mom came to take me home, and when she arrived, all I said to her was, "The Octopus." She understood.

It should not be a complete surprise then that ever since *Ecco the Dolphin*, ever since the Octopus, I've suffered from an enervating fear of the ocean, and to be honest, of all bodies of water bigger than a bathtub. Every summer, I embrace the popular wisdom and face my fear—I swim— and yet the fear never dissipates, the terror is always there. Only now am I beginning to understand that regardless of how many times I wade out into the water I will get no closer to the core of that fear, because the blanket on my friend's floor that threatened to swallow me up had little to do with the bay or the beach. The ocean that I fear is digital.

Let me explain.

After that first run-in with the Octopus, I hid the game cartridge at an unsuspecting friend's house, never to be seen again. I went right back to playing *Sonic*, where I could revel in skating across the surfaces of those death-trap oceans at supersonic speeds, impervious to the pull of their dark gravities. However, the longer I left helpless Ecco alone down there, the longer I clung to the cartoon physics that kept Sonic atop the water, the more I allowed the dominion of the Octopus to increase. Once my family migrated north, my direct experience of the ocean was mostly limited to an annual pilgrimage to Lido Beach on Long Island, and so over time, the "real" ocean grew less and less real, becoming a mere analogy for the digital. While I was off racing through corkscrews and loop-the-loops with my favorite blue hedgehog, the Cyber-Cephalopod was busy taking over Flushing Bay and Jones Beach, seizing the whole of the Atlantic; the reach of its tentacles soon extended to every unguarded and unconsidered body of water I had or might ever come across, digitizing them, converting their salt and foam to pixels and code, refashioning all-things-wet in the image of its 16-bit lair. Don't believe me? To this day I won't even go in a swimming pool alone. I don't know the limits of the Octopus's power, and I don't intend to test them.

Here's where I run into problems. As if chronic nightmares and beach anxiety weren't enough, this thalassophobia has kept me at a distance from environmentalism in any capacity, and now hinders my complete engagement with literary ecology. I wonder too whether allowing the ocean to function as a repository for my unconscious fears has had effects more sinister than the mere feeling of being excluded from the eco-party. By imagining the ocean as invincible, have I blinded myself to the existence of any real vulnerabilities the sea might possess? To the destructive effects of pollution, toxication, over-fishing? How can

I truly process ecological violence, knowing the Octopus is down there, biding his time, protected by all that invincible digital blue?

III

The world of video games has changed quite a bit since 1995. One of the advantages of internet-enabled consoles with large internal hard drives is that old cartridge-based games (which are miniscule by today's standards) can be downloaded directly to your system. There's no more need to dig through boxes in the attic if you want to wax nostalgic over a few rounds of *Punch Out!* or take a belated stab at *Shinobi III*—all it takes is a credit card and a wi-fi connection. I happen to know that *Ecco the Dolphin* is available for both the Nintendo Wii and Xbox 360 at this very moment.

The thing is, that in these almost twenty years since I first saw the Octopus, my own relationship with video games has changed as well. As a kid, I had trouble beating any game. I played for hours on end, more or less every day, but seldom was I disciplined (or talented?) enough to work my way through every level, every boss battle, all the way to the end credits—even in *Sonic the Hedgehog*. These days, I experience a legitimate sense of guilt when I abandon a game midway, and I make an honest effort not to buy games I know I won't have the time or patience to beat.

I'm unsure whether it's this new imperative to finish what I've started, or the fact that I've been filling my head with literary ecology—Timothy Morton's *strange stranger* and Donna Haraway's *companion species* come to mind—but as of late, I've noticed a shift in the way that I remember my first meeting with Octopus. Now I can't help but remember *Ecco the Dolphin* as another game I left unbeaten, and I've realized I have no idea who or what the Octopus represented *in the game*, to Ecco. Was it friend or foe? What did it want? Did I need to get past it, or was it moments away from bestowing upon Ecco some new ability or item when I panicked and shut down the system?

I will never forsake Sonic (even now, I'm plotting his rehabilitation as a bona fide eco-hero) but if I continue to insist on putting myself in his speedy red shoes, I run the risk of fearing the ocean forever, and any attempt I make to join the ecocritical conversation will be haunted by a fundamental hypocrisy. That's not to say I want to default to thinking of myself as a victim, pleading for pity, a little kid traumatized by the sight of a scary monster. Only that after so many years, it may be time to start thinking of myself *as* Ecco, to embrace the imperiled and uncertain mantle of this 16-bit dolphin who needs to figure out how to respond to the big orange octopus if he's going to beat the game.

The next time my family treks out to Lido Beach, I will sit among knots of seaweed and sun-fried jellyfish, and look out at the water. The ocean will be digital, and the Octopus will be out there—there's no helping that. But this year, when I hear theme music in the distance, when the title screen flashes on the horizon, I might Press Start.

A Short History of the
Hudsonian Ice Age

Nancy Nowacek and Lowell Duckert

to which is added
a guide/less/book for the erratic explorer
along with
essential queries and supply rosters

23986–11286 B.C.E.

G oing back to a river's beginning is not to pinpoint its source—it is to begin (again). Time may *flow*, but a river always escapes the trappings of chronology. Riparian time emphasizes riptides, eddies, and turbulent zones over lines, origins, and laminar points.

> (All we know are these confluences: Skype chats and emails; poetry and bridge sections; rivers and tides; bendable and multipliable time. Data streams, hover-craft, "Hudson," *Muhheakantuck*.)

How do we understand a body of water without our own—in it, with it, through it? What will be the stuff of this day's bridges—of space, time, conversation, question and experience— enlisted to build tomorrow's? Does the water outside my window know that I'm watching it, wondering where it will go next? Will it love as it is loved?

☐ Broadband connectivity
☐ Iced coffee
☐ In-box attachments
☐ NOAA charts
☐ Public Trust Doctrine
☐ Salt in the veins

April 10, 1815

Mount Tambora in the Dutch East Indies erupts, spreading its volcanic ash worldwide. Crops fail. Poverty soars. Europe, still in the grips of the Little Ice Age, deems 1816 the "Year Without Summer." "Seasonless, herbless, treeless, manless, lifeness": Byron's "Darkness."[1]

(Less is *more* to those on the volcanic rim, those who wonder why the end is deemed *nigh* with the arrival of particulate neighbors, born from the explosive earth. Even "a chaos of hard clay" shines light from its magmatic core. It is warm here.)

Will we soon be living Years Without Winter as some now live Years Without Water? When will ours come? Will the ice ever return? Would it want to?

☐ Stories of Pompeii
☐ Skates
☐ Yellow ochre
☐ Woolens
☐ Farmer's Almanac

1   *Selected Poetry of Lord Byron*, ed. Leslie A. Marchand (New York: Random House, 2001), 221.

Winter 1817

Temperatures reach -26 F (-32 C) in Upper New York Bay. Horse-drawn sleighs cross the frozen Buttermilk Channel to Governors Island.

> (Some fear that Hudson's ghost approaches from the northwest, recounting the river's chilling history as an imagined passageway to Asia. They feel what Arctic explorers felt: cold.)

What of Nature's ambivalence? Is what is perceived as cruelty merely necessary? Without summer, what then?

- ☐ Waxed boots
- ☐ Goggles
- ☐ Blankets
- ☐ Face mask
- ☐ Buckets
- ☐ Guns
- ☐ Pitiless determination

1784

Governors Island gets its name from the British royal governors who had reserved the island for their exclusive use, replacing "Noten Eylandt" ("Island of Nuts") given by the first settlers of New Netherland. The Native Americans had previously called the island "Paggank," or "Nut Island" due to the forests of nut-bearing trees that once flourished there. The state government currently recognizes Governors Island as the birthplace of New York City, lauding the "legal-political guaranty of tolerance onto the North

American continent"[2] proclaimed by the Dutch upon their landing in 1624.

> (Juan Rodgriguez, born in Santa Domingo from Portuguese and African parents and a translator for the Dutch, is the first documented non-native resident and arguably the first citizen of New York City. Arriving in 1613, he marries into the indigenous community and learns the Algonquian language. Tolerance can be a successful alternative to governance—regarding humans, trees, nuts—especially when it extends across the continent to a widening range of beings. An island cannot be governed, a channel's tides never wait; all relationships are fragile, every interaction precarious. No man owns an island.)

Is an island still an island if there's a bridge connecting it to mainland? Does it become something else? A satellite, fruit, or merely an accessory?

- ☐ Sandbar
- ☐ Canoe
- ☐ Paddle
- ☐ Satchel
- ☐ Beads
- ☐ Ribbons
- ☐ Kettle
- ☐ Epi-pen
- ☐ Eldridge Tide and Pilot
- ☐ A strong breaststroke

---

2   Resolutions No. 5476 and No. 2708: http://tolerancepark.org/id5.html.

Summer 2008

New York City Mayor Michael Bloomberg breaks ground on Governors Island, laying claim to the 150 acres sold by the federal government to the city and the State of New York in 2003. The Trust for Governor's Island promises a mix of recreational, educational, and hospitality services—"a park created by and for New Yorkers."[3] A new world is only a ferry ride away.

> (The Tolerance Park Foundation reveres Governors Island. Their proposed "living museum" to commemorate, they believe, the first legal declaration of religious tolerance in the New World—to be built by 2009, the quatercentenary of the Half Moon's arrival—never materialized.[4] Onboard a more modern vessel, landscape architects discuss a rising bay and the threats it poses to the Park and Public Space Master Plan,[5] perhaps listening to the objections water itself *raises* (from Old English *rīsan*—"make an attack, wake, get out of bed."). This voice asks who and what counts as *public*, who can afford to arrive, to stay, to return. To work with water's destabilizing effects, no one can reclaim what has been taken, only cohabit what has always been shared. An agency derived through nonhuman relation is a bridge between once-opposed worlds, a redefinition of citizenry, a wet wake up call.)

3   Updates are available on their website: http://www.govisland.com/ html/home/home. shtml.

4   Their initiative appears to be ongoing: http://www.tolerancepark.org/.

5   A detailed description of the plan is available here: http://www.west8. nl/projects/all/ governors_island/.

Does imagination grow bigger, richer, fuller, when it has land in which to root? How can the shipping chain learn tolerance for the public, patience for that which is not sold?

- ☐ Golden shovel & Commemorative plaques
- ☐ Paparazzi and PR agents
- ☐ Souvenir pens
- ☐ Life jackets
- ☐ Bullhorn
- ☐ Board of Directors
- ☐ Angel investors
- ☐ Business plan
- ☐ Patience

June 3, 1864

A quarter century before Walt Whitman reminisces about the sand bar across Buttermilk Channel, he writes dejectedly about a different dairy product in a letter to his mother. Taking care of wounded soldiers outside Washington, DC, during the Civil War, "I gave the boys in Carver hospital a great treat of ice cream a couple of days ago, went round myself through about 15 large wards, (I bought some ten gallons, very nice)—you would have cried & been amused too, many of the men had to be fed, several of them I saw cannot probably live, yet they quite enjoyed it."[6] Amidst the ghastliness of war, Whitman reaches out to his neighbors in an act of love—many unknown, one familiar—providing them with a moment of joy, even if it proves to be as ephemeral as ice on a hot summer day.

6   *Selected Letters of Walt Whitman*, ed. Edwin Haviland Miller (Iowa City: University of Iowa Press, 1990), 104.

(Hurricane Sandy wrecks infrastructures and stalls even the best-laid artistic plans. And it motivates them: an artist restarts her experiment in staying afloat during inter- and intra-catastrophic times, engineering a Citizen's Bridge bound by the physical buoyancy of objects and collaboration with others. A bridge that has contingency built-in, unpredictability expressed, destruction pre-determined. There is no perceivable point across the bridge—just the company of the present and its *building* potential. "Let 'be' be finale of seem."[7] Let love be in times of strife.)

Can enough frozen cream, melted, flood the belly? Where is the ice cream in a flood?

- ☐ Vanilla
- ☐ Cream
- ☐ Sugar
- ☐ Salt
- ☐ Buckets
- ☐ Cranks
- ☐ Gauze
- ☐ Scoop
- ☐ Spoons
- ☐ Bowls
- ☐ Penicillin

7   Wallace Stevens, "The Emperor of Ice Cream," in *The Collected Poems of Wallace Stevens* (New York: Vintage Books, 1990), 64.

September 26, 2013

We meet at Oceanic New York and decide that our bridges should intersect, thus beginning our erratic expedition together.

January 7, 2014

New York City records a temperature of 3 F (-16 C) as the Polar Vortex sweeps south from the Arctic Circle. Up to twelve inches of ice form on the Hudson River, prompting the US Coast Guard to deploy icebreakers in order to keep shipping lanes open.

> (At several times during the nineteenth century, New Yorkers perilously walked across "ice bridges" along the East and Hudson Rivers for a variety of reasons. Ice floes carried away several curious people on the former in 1857, while in 1821 a temporary tavern was built on the latter. As a substance in-between liquid and solid, melting and freezing, ice bridges *bridge* connections between things as well as distribute them: a warmth of a drink shared with a fellow brave citizen can lead to a life-threatening ride atop an iceberg, or even a thrilling one inside an ice yacht, popular on the Hudson since the late nineteenth century. Ice moves, and ice moves us. If there is no governor (or emperor) of ice, only citizens, if there is no central organization to the public, only bridges that span both local and global, then let Hudson be your guide: to err is non/human; and to tolerate, not just in the sense of patiently enduring pain (Latin *tolerare*), but in sharing the burden of endurance with another in order to lessen its hardship, *humane*.)

How does one establish stability on an ice bridge? With the razor edge of a skate or the point of a pick axe? Does water always—no matter its form—counter balance, or is the real adversary time?

☐ Sand
☐ Extra scarf
☐ Extra socks
☐ Hood
☐ Hat
☐ Earmuffs
☐ Gray piles of garbage, oil, and iced slush
☐ Caution

1966

Between 1947 and 1997, General Energy dumped an estimated 1.3 million pounds of polychlorinated biphenyls (PCBs) into the Hudson River (the public). Pete and Toshi Seeger start Hudson River Sloop Clearwater in 1966 to protest the river's contamination.[8]

> (One of the last songs Pete wrote (with Lorre Wyatt) was recorded onboard a vessel of the same name in 2012. "It's time to turn things around / Trickle up, not trickle down," he sings, "Hopin' we'll all pull through."[9] It is a chorus writ with water.)

8   For more on the organization's dedication to environmental justice, visit: http://www.clearwater.org/.

9   "God's Counting on Me, God's Counting on You."

Who owns the water? And what of when 'navigation' means hoisting anchors for a vessel made of rafts? How does one walk against four knots?

- ☐ 50-gallon drums
- ☐ Ratchet straps
- ☐ Power drill & drywall screws
- ☐ Spreadsheets and emails
- ☐ 2×4s
- ☐ Plywood sheets
- ☐ Nets & U-bolts
- ☐ Naval Engineering
- ☐ A firm handshake
- ☐ Unending curiosity
- ☐ Leaps of faith
- ☐ Courage for ignored correspondence
    and cancelled meetings

Summer 2014–

Like Whitman's *Leaves of Grass* (1900), we take in "[t]he summer air" of "Mannahatta," only to think on boreal winds in the next breath: "The winter snows, the sleigh-bells—the broken ice in the river, passing along, up or down, with the flood tide or ebb-tide."[10]

How long? When exactly? What final requirements and costs for twenty-first–century bodies to relearn the river's? What channels will bridge agendas, world-views, and political

---

10   *Complete Poetry and Selected Prose* (New York: Literary Classics of the United States, 1982), 613.

tides? Can we choose to be for something else instead of against another?

☐ A new definition of progress
☐ Recalibration of success
☐ A universe of things
☐ Harnessed fricton
☐ Reverberant creativity
☐ Hope

(We would sing these songs of shared selves in future.)

Wages of Water

Steve Mentz

This fragment has two parts. The first splashes through the Hudson River one early morning in September 2013. The second took place that same fall, on the Monday before Thanksgiving, inside the canal of my left ear.

In diving into the "wages" of water I'm not suggesting that the world ocean owes us anything. Nor really the opposite, that we owe the great waters a globe without plastic, or with less carbon, much as I love such fanciful ideas. (To clarify: we are heading for a lower-carbon future. The question is whether we'll burn all the coal and oil in the ground before we get there. That's what will determine the shape of our catastrophic future.) The wages I'm talking in this case about are personal. Not an ocean inside, though part of this story takes place inside my body. What I'm writing about is salt on skin, the feel and pressure of the world ocean on a fragile individual body, in this case mine. How does it feel, I ask, to touch the hyperobject?

Ecological catastrophe becomes legible as a matter of scale. Carbon fills the two flowing bodies that cover our planet's surface, the wet one and the airy one. It's hard to pinpoint one source for all that industrial by-product, but New York will do. The city's story—colonization, urban growth, industrial expansion, post-industrial "knowledge economy," punctuated collapses and recoveries—maps onto the history of what Tim Morton terms the "age of catastrophes." I don't fully agree with the lingering Romanticism of Morton's two points of origin, the invention of the steam engine in 1781, and the detonation of the first atomic bomb in 1945, since humanity's carbon signature appears legible for around ten thousand years, but I do agree with the conceptual potency of his powerful neologism, the hyperobject. More than human-sized, massively distributed, everywhere present if not always quite tangible, hyperobjects come into view as the massive shadow of global warming and catastrophic climate change. In this twilight it's hard to distinguish individuals. Claims for human exceptionalism ring false. Nonhuman forces control our future.

But I'm still me, for all that. A body simply body, however vast and rambling my thoughts. I grew up close to New York and teach in Queens now. There's something about language and consciousness that doesn't like to give up the I.

These two stories narrate my physical and intellectual efforts to come to terms with global warming and with Oceanic New York. In the first I'm in the water, and in the second it's in me. In the spirit of adventure stories, you'll have to wait until the end to see how it turns out.

1. Flotsam

At 4:04 A.M. at the Battery on Saturday 26 September 2013, the tide turned. An instant of stillness—though nothing remains still in the water—and then the flood came, and the vast Atlantic started rolling up the Hudson. By high tide at 10:09 A.M., the water level at the Battery was 5.7 feet higher than it had been six hours before.

But by that time I was upriver, flotsam in the current, swimming north.

I jumped into the water at the 79th St. Boat Basin just before 8 A.M. I swam north for five miles, aiming for the Manhattan stanchion of the George Washington Bridge and the Little Red Lighthouse in its shadow. Passing under the span, I reached land near the northern tip of the island at the Dyckman Street Marina. I finished in 2:14:10. The winning time was 1:38.

Long distance swims are solitary events, spent mostly with your face underwater. I went out with the second wave and, feeling good in my new sleeveless wetsuit, soon caught many swimmers from the first wave. There may have been a moment, say around 8:30 A.M. when I caught a glimpse of the tower of Riverside Church at 121st St., when I may have been near the front of the pack. Then a bunch of fast swimmers who started behind me surged ahead at the bridge, and I finished in a crowd.

I'd never swum that far in that strong a current before. The flood was behind me, which was better than the alternative but meant that the ocean was crawling up my back all morning, sloppy surges tickling my legs, shifting me off-keel. Travelling north were millions of gallons of salt water, me, two hundred seventeen other swimmers, maybe thirty kayaks, fifteen larger boats, twenty NYPD zodiacs, and a dozen blue-capped "Swim Angels," who were there to help anyone in trouble. It didn't seem at all crowded at first.

All that fast-moving water and debris meant turbulence. I swam through constant movement: little waves pushing upriver, eddies, wakes from powerboats which left us tasting gasoline. Maybe halfway, with the Bridge not looking much closer, I started to feel seasick.

Long swims mix exertion with meditation. Diana Nyad calls swimming the "ultimate form of sensory deprivation." I remember a wordless feeling, flowing forward with flowing water. *Mobilis in mobili* is what Captain Nemo calls it, mobility inside a moving thing. For a little while that morning, I was part of the biggest moving thing in New York. Inside what Tim Morton calls "the mesh," surrounded by a moving environment that buoyed me up and threatened me at the same time, swimming seemed part fool's errand and part deep-down encounter with reality. Humans aren't aquatic.

But when you're in the big river, heading upstream with the flood, and your arms and legs move machine-like, and you're churning upstream with New York City on your right and the Palisades on your left, you feel in your disoriented body why "flow" is a good thing to be inside.

2. Excess

The knife entered my ear canal deliberately on the Monday before Thanksgiving. It moved down three-quarters of an inch until it encountered two lumps of bone. These bone masses narrowed my ear canal as rocky headlands narrow an estuary. A passage that was ten millimeters wide constricted with these bone-headlands to a single millimeter. That's where the knife started cutting.

The skin peeled back in still-attached flaps, flooding the canal with blood and exposing bare bone. The drill started there. Several hours later, the extruding bone was gone.

The bone-headlands grew and made that narrowness because of exposure to water. A lifetime of immersion in oceans, lakes, and rivers, cold water-fingers flowing into my ear canal up to the eardrum. Water didn't go away when it got inside my head. It lingered, thick and heavy, an alien presence inside my skull. Eventually it flowed out—but for a long time, the insides of my ears have been intermittently wet. I've been living with a little salt ocean in my head.

There is a moral to this story.

We love oceans, but they don't love us. We're semi-aquatic apes who can't endure the excess of ocean. Swimmers feel it: the water is no place to stay.

After the surgery, I wasn't able to put my head under any water for over three months. Not until the next spring.

Two Sublimes

Steve Mentz

1. The Dry
(thinking about Lucretius)

When I tried to count the rings the next day
I estimated one hundred years.
Numbers create order, and I sought precision:
    40 feet tall
    60 inches around at my chest's height
    20 inches in diameter.
    1913.
The tree had been, for a century, the highest point in
       Short Beach,
O'ertopping the church steeple that started its ascent
       partway down the hill.
It came down in the dark.
I was sitting on the couch with the kids reading about
       Fangorn Forest.
Eald enta geworc.
We heard a sound
Whoosh
And a harsh clatter of wires yanked from shingles.

We stared into darkness, seeing nothing
Because there was nothing to see.
Olivia understood first what the faint glimmer and
        emptiness meant:
"The pine tree," she said.
"It's gone."

2. The Wet
        (thinking about Longinus)

When the hurricane made landfall I went outside
To play a game of chance with overhead wires and
        windswirl.
I could not help myself.
I walked down the street to a granite ridge overlooking
        the water.
I stood there next to my neighbor, a man who makes his
        living building houses.
We watched as rows of waves like hump-backed rams
Shouldered their way, sloppy and frothing, onto shore.
We saw water splattering onto and through our
        neighbors' homes,
Erupting high and foamy into white cloud-fragments,
Scattering sand and salt and wood and drywall into
        the surf.
"Isn't it beautiful?"
Is what he said to me.

The Water is Rising

The second selection of nine essays opens up
flooded streets to global connections.
Steve Mentz and Marina Zurkow conspire
on instructions for flooded cities.
Jeffrey Jerome Cohen reveals
the sea's conveying motions.
Allan Mitchell plunges down
into oceanic and poetic forms.
Dean Kritikos invites Jean-Paul Sartre
and Timothy Morton to visit
his hometown of New York City.
Anne Harris values depth, uncertainty, and disaster.
Julie Orlemanski explores
what it would take to move
from tourism to activism.
Jonathan Hsy slides into
the watery basis of
language and metaphor.
Nancy Nowacek narrates
her epic story of
bridging Buttermilk Channel.
Jeffrey Jerome Cohen
and Allan Mitchell
exchange dispatches
about the ocean
from opposite sides
of a continent.

Instructions
In Case of Immersion

Steve Mentz and Marina Zurkow

What skills or habits do we need to live in an Oceanic City? Swimmers might want to set themselves down naked, like Hamlet after his pirate adventure, but the more usual way for humans to live in oceanic space is with tools. Life buoys are not just metaphors. Think about the oldest sea-survivor, the man with the many twists and turns, polymetic and polytropic. Even when he's naked in the water, he's full of tools: prayers to the grey-eyed GPS, gift-exchange of Ino's magic veil, flirting with Nausicaa. Sails and ropes aren't the only things that help sailors float.

We lack Odysseus's tools. No goddess seems to be listening. No non-celluloid princess is doing their washing nearby. I've misplaced my magic veil. The tools we need, we need to make ourselves. We need bridges and poems and life-boats. I wouldn't personally want to cram everyone into an ark, no matter how roomy inside. The idea of oceanic living isn't to escape the sea but to engage it.

Buoyancy is important. The five bare fathoms near the surface are just a tiny fragment of the great god Ocean's big body, but those surface fathoms, light-filtered, are where we can survive. This essay proposes some ways to live in a flooded environment.

It's temporary stuff. Land animals like us don't do well long-term in the water, minor exceptions like the Bajau Laut or "sea gypsies" of Malaysia, or Melville's silent hero Bulkington notwithstanding. But what's not temporary?

These Instructions offer six maxims and two pictures as ways to live in a flooding plain.

1   To make floodlands into pastoral spaces you need to add poets. and shepherds. How exactly do we make sure that everyone sings together?

2   Look closely at all asphalt borders: curbs, potholes, parking spaces, driveways. The way in is the same as the way out. If you need to, or if you want to, get down on your belly to look more closely. You'll see the water leaking out if you look close enough.

3   The best way—the only way?—to make soft edges out of squares is to apply friction. Lots of friction. It's painful stuff. Especially if you're still down there on your belly.

Figure 1: Where to keep your boat.
It's important that it be ready-to-hand.
Just on the other side of the air-conditioner.

4   Look at the Newtown Creek and smell History.

5   Think about this: if you are floating in an
     inflatable raft in Buttermilk Channel during a
     hundred-year-flood, and you're blowing as hard
     as you can into a little plastic nozzle in order
     to keep the raft full and buoyant and above the
     water which is itself rising, your efforts match
     two fluid flows against each other. The basic
     ideas is to use the flow of air from your lungs
     into the cavity of the raft to counter the flow of
     salt water into New York Harbor that's raising
     the Channel. It might be possible to use the little
     flow to counter the bigger flow, for a little while.

6   Drowning, as Sebastian Junger explains in *The
     Perfect Storm*, is a form of radical experimenta-
     tion with a watery environment. The drowning
     swimmer flounders up against the "Zero-Limit
     Point." "Holidng our breath is killing us," Junger
     reasons the body might say to itself when under-
     water for too long, "and breathing in might not
     kill us, so we might as well breathe in."[1]

     He's describing Oceanic New York as much as
     George Clooney.

---

1   Sebastian Junger, *The Perfect Storm: A True Story of Men against
     the Sea*, (New York: W.W. Norton, 1997) 142.

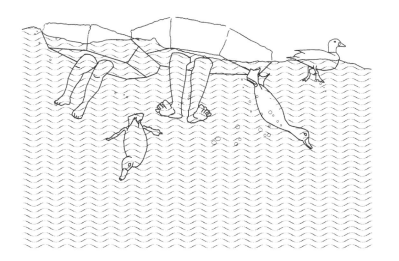

Figure 2: The view from below.
If we had eyes in the soles of our feet,
we'd see what the ducks see.

The Sea is a Conveyance-Machine

Jeffrey Jerome Cohen

a waterlog

I. Convoys

"**T**here came over them the hosts of Portugal to destroy and to exterminate all that is called Israel, children and women in one day."[1] So wrote Isaac Aboab in the first Hebrew poem of the Americas, around 1649. Aboab composed this text in Recife, destined to become a city of Brazil but at the time capital of a fleeting entity called Nieuw-Holland. The port was under siege by the Portuguese, determined to destroy the Jewish community sheltered there. Born to Marranos fleeing religious persecution, Isaac Aboab and his family had dwelled for a while in France, practicing a reclaimed Judaism. To avoid forced return to Christianity their community migrated to Amsterdam, and then to South America, and to peril.

To destroy and to exterminate all that is called Israel. In naval convoy the Inquisition reaches the port of Recife, intent on obliteration. Isaac Aboab fashions a poem of

---

1   "Zekher Asiti le-Nifle'ot El," in M. Kayserling, "Isaac Aboab, the First Jewish Author in America," *Publications of the American Jewish Historical Society* (1897): 125–36, accessed http://jawutrecht.files. wordpress.com/2012/11/out-26.pdf

difficult transit, then sails with his family to transatlantic
refuge. Excavating the fragmentary details of Aboab's
biography in 1897, M. Kayserling deploys a marine trope
to capture this hazardous voyaging, edged by liquidation:
"The terrors of war overwhelmed him and his followers,
who had been cast upon a strange land as by waves of the
ocean."[2] Aboab lived a long life after his Amsterdam return.
Other members of his shattered community, however,
boarded a French ship out of Recife and sailed for the
small village of New Amsterdam. Twenty-three arrived on
the island of Manhattan in 1654. Peter Stuyvesant, Director-
General of the Colony of New Netherland, attempted their
immediate eviction, but the Dutch West India Company
countermanded. Most departed across the water before
a new surge of immigrants rechristened the region New
York. Yet by the end of the century Manhattan had its first
synagogue, Shearith Israel ("Remnant of Israel"), a Sephar-
dic congregation intimately connected to Europe and the
Caribbean. New members arrived in frequent ships.

To this day New York City contains the largest
Jewish population in the United States, about a third of
the country's total.[3] Few think of the Jews as a sea-going
people, perhaps, but long Diaspora is proof enough of
maritime intimacy, littoral affinities. *Esē diaspora en pasais
basileias tēs gēs,* "thou shalt be a dispersion in all kingdoms

---

2   M. Kayserling, "Isaac Aboab, the First Jewish Author in America,"
    127. Further on Aboab's life and works see Alexander Altmann, *Von
    der mittelalterlichen zur modernen Aufklärung: Studien zur jüdischen
    Geistesgeschichte* (Tübingen: Mohr Siebeck, 1987), 206–7.

3   For a brief history of Jewish New York, see Lance J. Sussman, "New
    York Jewish History" http://www.4uth.gov.ua/usa/english/society/
    religion/jewhist.htm

of the earth."[4] The sea is precarious transport, a waterway
that gathers Portugal, France, Brazil, the Netherlands, New
York into meshworked crossings. The North Atlantic Gyre:
ships traverse the same pelagic conveyor belt that carries
Saharan storms to American coasts as an obliteration of
hurricanes. These ships return (if they return) through the
same compulsion of currents, the Gulf Stream and North
Atlantic Drift, pressing tropic waters to European chill. The
Atlantic is a vortex chain, a gearwork for marine conveyance: bodies, goods, ships, words.

He did not name himself. Isaac Aboab, first to write
enduring Hebrew along a shore that did not become
home, bears a surname in which is evident linguistic
whorls. "Aboab" is a name found only among the Jews of
Spain and Portugal. It is Arabic in origin (perhaps from
abdelwahab, "father benefactor"). "Aboab" intersects—
sonorously, etymologically, obliquely—with Hebrew "Ahab"
(אֲחְאָב, "father's brother"). A famously wayward king of
Israel, Ahab worshipped Baal, spurned the prophets, died
in battle, had his blood licked by dogs. A famously errant
seafarer, another Ahab captained a ship that was a hard
trope. Christened for an exterminated people, bearing in
its name a story of liquidation, the Pequod was a polyglot
vessel, transportation in multiple genres that in its founder-
ing showed the truth of travel in *travail*. Words disperse
along spirals of etymology, convoys of narrative transit
bound for new shores or catastrophe. *All that most mad-
dens and torments; all that stirs up the lees of things; all
truth with malice in it…*

Oceanic New York is a confluence, a space of crossings where in fits and starts a literature of many tongues

4   Septuagint version of Deuteronomy, 28:25.

emerges, an archive of marine poiesis. Because at times the
ocean transports and at times swallows, because the sea is
trope and material turning [*trepein*]—inward, downward
or towards obliteration—it is difficult to say what stories
will endure, what soundings will resound. *Hazardous*, from
Middle English and Old French (*hasard*), from Spanish
(*azar*), from Arabic (*az-zahr*). The gyred Atlantic scatters
the enclosed Mediterranean, a whirl of flows for convoys.
Current-crossed and relentless, the froth and flux of oceans
bear shipwreck, effacement, a bare record of receding
wakes, a cobbled fleet of appositions, words and things.

Convoy, convey, convoke: the way together, or
together voiced.

II. Confluence

"I say to you, Put wax in your ears rather against the hungry
sea / it is not our home!"[5] When currents convey storms
and savage waves as well as ships and savage tropes, the
sea devours. Abyssal depths are silence and forgetting. Of
marine hazard Steve Mentz writes eloquently:

> [The sea] is the place on earth that remains inimical
> to human life…The most fundamental feature of the
> ocean, for poets, scientists, fishermen, and swimmers
> alike, is neither its immutable form nor its vastness
> but its inhospitality.[6]

5   William Carlos William, *Paterson* (New York: New Directions, 1992), 200.

6   *At the Bottom of Shakespeare's Ocean* (London: Continuum, 2009), 5.
    Mentz's formulation of a "blue cultural studies" and a "swimmer
    poetics" here and in his capacious scholarship has been essential to
    my own work.

The sea is hostile to human life, and a trigger to human thriving. No less spurred to poetry than William Carlos Williams, Mentz quietly limns his fine description of saltwater inhospitality with the work of those who take from the hungry deep their sustenance, "poets, scientists, fishermen, and swimmers." The ocean wrecks, engulfs, pulls to cold oblivion. To navigate its hazardous provision and sublime excess you must—like the sailors who companioned Odysseus—stop your ears against its invitation to swim, to swallow, to cease. But the ocean also fosters: a bounty of whales, fish, crustaceans, shells, stories, transport, lyric, metaphor. Esurient, unaccommodating, nothing like a home, the ocean allures, buoys, preserves, saturates. Its shanties trace the littoral between prosperity and despair, sustenance and starvation, song and silence, appositional gyres.

Peregrine Horden and Nicholas Purcell map how the Mediterranean has over the millennia gathered long coasts, small islands, and heterogeneous microclimates into human unity, a space for fluctuating mobilities and enduring transport, military and commercial.[7] What we persist in labeling "the Earth's Middle" [*medius + terra*],

7   *The Corrupting Sea: A Study of Mediterranean History* (Oxford: Blackwell Publishers, 2000). Horden and Purcell aim to extend the work of Fernand Braudel, *The Mediterranean and the Mediterranean World in the Age of Phillip II*, trans. Sian Reynolds, 2 vols. (New York: Harper & Row, 1976). See the thorough appraisal and detailed explication their ongoing project in Suzanne Conklin Akbari, "The Persistence of Philology: Language and Connectivity in the Mediterranean," *A Sea of Languages: Rethinking the Arabic Role in Medieval Literary History*, ed. Suzanne Conklin Akbari and Karla Mallette (Toronto: University of Toronto Press, 2013), 3–22.

that omphalos of an ocean, centers shifting terrain.[8] Its
tumult of languages provide durable vocabulary for
navigating waters and narratives.[9] Deluge, deforestation,
earthquake, ash, and landslide are so constant as to be
unremarkable, so that to the Mediterranean belongs "an
environmental history without catastrophe" (*Corrupting
Sea* 338). Whether human or ecological, "little or nothing
is permanent" (339). Perhaps when poet-voyagers like Isaac
Aboab sailed to Atlantic shores (Amsterdam, Brazil, New
York) they conveyed the imprint of diurnal catastrophe, a
language of sea-swallow, wreck and story's ruin released on
less bounded shores.[10]

8   Through a comparative analysis David Abulafia foregrounds the
    sea as a mechanism for cultural intermixture in a way that Horden
    and Purcell do not in his essay "Mediterraneans," *Rethinking the
    Mediterranean*, ed. W. V. Harris (Oxford: Oxford University Press,
    2005), 64–93. His emphasis on ocean as a kind of verb resonates with
    Stuart Elden's recent work on territory as process, "made and remade,
    shaped and shaping, active and reactive" (*The Birth of Territory*
    [Chicago: University of Chicago Press, 2013]), 17.

9   I am thinking especially here of Jonathan Hsy's work on the ocean
    as linguistic connective space in *Trading Tongues: Merchants,
    Multilingualism, and Medieval Literature* (Columbus: Ohio State
    University Press, 2013) and Sebastian Sobecki on the sea as a connective
    space across which tropes slide from one genre to another in *The Sea and
    Medieval English Literature* (Cambridge: D. S. Brewer, 2008).

10 Amsterdam would be part of the "Mediterranean of the North," a
    designation used by Robert S. Lopez, *The Commercial Revolution of
    the Middle Ages, 950–1350* (Cambridge: Cambridge University Press,
    1976) to link Scandinavia, Britain, Germany, and Flanders with the
    Baltic. "Mediterranean Atlantic" could describe Brazil's situation,
    and is from Felipe Fernández-Armesto, *Before Columbus: Exploration
    and Colonization from the Mediterranean to the Atlantic, 1229–1492*
    (Philadelphia: University of Pennsylvania Press, 1987). Such multiple
    Mediterraneans are at the heart of Abulafia's argument, which
    emphasizes dynamic interconnection of a kind that can render even

Barry Cunliffe collects the seaboard sweeps of the
Atlantic and the roiling of its cold waters into a similarly
turbulent community.[11] This ocean likewise fosters contact
(war and trade), desire (for voyage, for distant goods
and bodies), communication (stories, shanties, poems, a
saltwater lingua franca to resound across small and landed
dialects). Resisting the scholarly habit of isolating geographies into linguistic differences and brief chronological
spans, Cunliffe maps how the shared experience of dwelling at a marine verge sustained vast, connective flows over
long durations. But an ocean is more than a medium for
human collectivity, more than a force for fashioning some
universal pidgin of whorls. Aqueous matter is history-rich
metaphor, a marine-poetic transport mechanism that runs
in many directions at once, sometimes in perilous cascade.
Across spiraling planes (current, conveyance) as well as
through vertical engulfment (drowning, oblivion), the
ocean is transport and catastrophe.

All scatt'red in the bottom of the sea. Hazard the waters
as you will, plumb the depths with fervor, and nothing
static responds. *What dreadful noise of waters in mine ears.*
A dream of death by drowning, a sounding of poetry on
the seafloor.

---

a desert a kind of ocean ("Mediterraneans"). Oceanic space is, in his
account, always unbounded.

11   Barry Cunliffe, *Facing the Ocean: The Atlantic and Its Peoples, 8000
BC–AD 1500* (Oxford: Oxford University Press, 2001). Cunliffe has
also written on the fluidity enabled through a multi-ocean nexus in
Europe Between the Oceans: Themes and Variations, 9000 BC–AD 1000
(New Haven: Yale University Press, 2008). I have examined Cunliffe's
work previously in my introduction to *Cultural Diversity in the British
Middle Ages: Archipelago, Island, England,* ed. Jeffrey Jerome Cohen
(New York: Palgrave Macmillan, 2008), 4.

III. Who by water

The long Jewish history of New York begins with the
community Isaac Aboab abandoned, a chronicle of
troubled sea voyage, and a chronicle of seas of trouble.
A few weeks before I spoke a version of what you now
read to a gathering of fellow navigators in Queens, Jews
throughout the world gathered in synagogues and twice
recited Unetanneh Tokef, a litany of catastrophes to
come:

> Who shall perish by water and who by fire?
> Who by tremor and who in plague?
> Who by suffocation and who by stone?
> Who shall have rest? Who shall wander?

Unetanneh Tokef humbles me, and not because I believe
in God; this world offers sufficient seas of trouble. But in
a time of anthropogenic climate change and superstorms
that obliterate, of death by fire and death by water, any
poem of apocalypse rings true. Yet I prefer Leonard
Cohen's 1974 version of the *piyyut*. His song is cheeky
in its secularity, poignant in its wonder, heavy in meta-
phoric transports:

> Who in these realms of love, who by something blunt,
> And who by avalanche, who by powder,
> Who for his greed, who for his hunger,
> And who shall I say is calling?

The telephone of that insouciant last line brings to
present interrogation a distant voice. A transatlantic call?
A trans-temporal message conveyed through the soon to

be lost technology of a landline? Or a failure of communi-cation, story not transported, a wrong number, try again?[12]

"I say to you, Put wax in your ears rather against the hungry sea / it is not our home!" But even if you fail to stop your ears against the sea's hungry song, even if your shanties cannot drown the pull, know that to be swallowed by waves is not always an oblivion. The sirens fashion their drums from the ribs and stretched skin of the drowned. Bones to coral, eyes to pearls. You may suffocate in the brine. You may sink to depths beyond recovery. But you may also become a material-historic conveyance device for the resounding of maritime tropes, metaphors, poetry, songs and stories—the literal become littoral.[13] An intermingling or material-linguistic crosscurrent. The anthropologist Alphonso Lingis describes an organism as a failure of solitude, "a dense and self-maintaining plenum" that takes energies from its environment, to transform and release as forces and passions.[14] This flux far surpasses the bare requirements of survival, so that every creature is an apparatus for the production of excess. Organisms in this way imitate their environments, which are themselves

> full of free and nonteleological energies—trade winds and storms, oceans streaming over three-fourths of the planet, drifting continental plates, cordilleras of

12   This series of questions is inspired by the brilliant work of Richard Burt and Julian Yates in *What's the Worst Thing You Can Do to Shakespeare?* (New York: Palgrave Macmillan, 2013), especially 17–45.

13   On the soundings that enable such littoral transport see Allen Mitchell's contribution to this volume.

14   *Dangerous Emotions* (Berkeley: University of California Press, 2000), 2.

the deep that erupt in volcanic explosions, and miles-deep glaciers piled up on Antarctica that flow into the sea and break off in bobbling icemountains (2).

Lingis composed these lines while wandering Easter Island, not New York. They suggest, however, that every organism conveys littorally: takes water, air, minerals into itself and releases its own vitality, sometimes as art or story. But as the New York's confluences make clear, some organisms release the toxic leavings of landed things: chemical detritus, a flow of poison the sea swallows but cannot obliterate. Stories are easier to liquidate than refuse.

Despite tempests, rogue waves, massacre and extermination, despite long stretches of hungry sea, some stories convey. Isaac Aboab left a poem to link Portugal, Brazil, Manhattan, Europe, a vector of water-clasp. His friends reached the Hudson without him. What of the Lenape, people who held New York before Europeans and their bacterial companions arrived? Lenape voices are more difficult to hear in oceanic New York, but sometimes they resound. Their Hudson was *Muhheakantuck*, a river that flows in two directions, a coming that is a going.[15] Back farther now still. The lower Hudson is a material text inscribed by twelve thousand years of human habitation, long thriving at the land's verge. Estuaries and shorelines convey bodies, connect buildings, engender lasting flows, matter-device for story. Some tales are the recovery of archeology, others a diligence for linguists. Most are swallowed. Some linger as wake.

Convoys transport more than humans. What of animals, timber, trade goods, parasites, stowaways, ballast and anchors? What of oceans not made of brine?

15   See Lowell Duckert's and Jonathan Hsy's contributions to this volume.

IV. Stone is slow water

The earliest humans in what is for the moment called New York hunted mastodons, timber wolves, and giant beavers. They knew the grate of glaciers, water solidified into hard conveyance. Wander Central Park and eventually you will arrive at ancient grey stone, bare mounds around which the landscape arranges. These are outcroppings of Manhattan Schist, 450 million years old. The grooves cut deep into their surface are glacial inscription, water-text etched when ice slid their surface. Jamie Kruse and Elizabeth Ellsworth call what unfolds in such moments of encounter "geopoetry," the meeting of story-obsessed witness with a "repository of mineral intelligence."[16] *Unfractioned idiom*, that writing of stones.

Panta rhei. Glacial text on New York's stone do not announce that rock rests immobile while even solid water flows. Manhattan Schist dates from the formation of Pangaea, perhaps the sixth supercontinent to have formed and dispersed. Oceanic New York becomes a geologic New York, and continents become conveyance-machines of their own. Earth and water together demand an elemental New York. Matter and metaphor mix. We are mineral and aqueous excrescences, airy breath and fiery heat, a transport device for the fourfold elements in their wandering. Earth, air, fire and water are makers, story triggers, an ebb and a flow and a vanishing.

And obscure as that heaven of the Jews / Thy guerdon. Or at least your shanty's end.

16 Jamie Kruse and Elizabeth Ellsworth, *Geologic City: A Field Guide to the GeoArchitecture of New York* (New York: smudge studio, 2011), sites 7 and 8.

Nine Soundings

Allan Mitchell

1

D redging up the tangled, toxic, ruined histories of nearby estuaries, *Silent Beaches, Untold Stories: New York City's Forgotten Waterfront* stands as a powerful rebuttal to the giddy industrial sublime of Hart Crane's *The Bridge*. Crane repudiated the pessimism of Eliot's *The Waste Land*, and erected an American epic in its place. But perhaps he was drowning not waving.

2

Those literary animadversions can seem worlds away from the wasted littoral on exhibit in fall 2013. So much background noise. But that noise recollects the nauseous complicity of sound and silence, story and sea, and how the ocean's measures and counter-measures have always threatened to confound and enchant. Tides keep their own time and, at a quicker pace, the waves beat across them at intervals, producing an arrhythmic swash and backwash on shore. A watery music. In *Works and Days* Hesiod refers to "measures of the loud-roaring seas," maritime *metra* whose waves are made to curl on the tongue. Homer's Odysseus is set upon an "unmeasured" (*ametretos*) sea journey that becomes epic. A deliberate and perverse paradox: the seas act as solvent to sense even as they demand epic feats of sense-making in neat hexameters.

3

We are at sea! All is protean! Writing these remarks I would have liked to avoid clichés but language itself is drenched with a liquid cognizance, words waterlogged. The ocean swirls, churns, turning up castaway utterances and elegiac laments, heroic exploits, and ordinary place-name that survive as seaborne reminiscences—from Flushing ("flowing place") to Skagway ("rough seas"). Geography and humanity together compose a raucous sea shanty.

4

Pelagic catastrophes are commonplaces too. We continue to imagine acts of seething, frothing, roaring seas: shades of Homer's "angry ocean" or Joyce's "cold mad feary father" at the end of *Finnegans Wake*. Linguistic edifices crumble as quickly as they are built. Chaucer's *House of Fame* articulates a devastating theory of human sense-making by analogy with emanating ripples of disturbed water, spreading outwards to become loud as waves beating upon rocks. Everything uttered ends in aqueous-cacophonous thrum, tumble, and crash.

5

Michel Serres observes that the noise of the ocean is
exactly, etymologically akin to the nausea associated
with oceangoing. Nautical noise: a seasick recognition of
fluid indifference perhaps; a felt sense of marine vastness
over and through which small human bodies continually
pass; an unbearable situation that provokes generations
of human intelligence to take the clamor of the seas for
murmurs or rumors, tides for tidings. We look for wave
patterns.

6

Epic has remained oceanic from Homer to Virgil and Ovid
on down to Charles Olson and Derek Walcott. A mascu-
line hydromythology springs eternal. Callamachus wrote
with Homer's epic sensibility in mind: "I do not admire
the bard who does not sing as much as the sea," referring
to the seaman-poet who is able to compose a maritime
music as expansive and moving as the ocean. As if the sea
itself were some superfluity that would overflow in song,
and become intelligible or navigable or tolerable thereby.
Walcott explicitly identifies poetry and seafaring in *Omeros*,
speaking of the "I" as the mast and the desk as a raft foaming with paper...His odyssey happens when "dipping the
beak / of a pen in its foam," as though the craft of poetry
were his watercraft. Or seabird.

7

The sea has long been synonymous with mythos, forms of
speaking or narrating. But standing at the limits of speech
and good sense too, many myths found at or below sea
level tend to be about turbid chaos, the abyss, the primary
element, the apeiron. And in this aspect the oceanic does
not so much speak as noisily sound and resound the
shallows of right thinking, straight paths, and male potency.
Wet Neptune seduces Leander in the Hellespont. Aphrodite
Anadyomene rises up from foaming remains of a castrated
sky god. Fortune comes in the form of tempestuous
passion and ruination. Leviathan lurks.

8

All of which leads me to ask, what is the song or story
of a depleted, polluted, littered ocean? It is a question of
poetry once again and of what is found and founders in
the depths. The flotsam and jetsam on exhibit—the glass
bottles, bones, ceramic, and other detritus of Dead Horse
Bay, the rotting furniture, spoiled food, old clothes, used
needles, and condoms of the notorious Gowanus Canal,
plus the many unseen chemical pollutants (pesticides, fuels,
metals, sewage)—rises to indict our ignorance and demand
better intelligences.

9

Literary history suggests that sea stories are just as much found as made, which makes me think that more beach-combing is just what is required. The eco-catastrophes portended by our wastes may tempt another epic poet to sing of great cosmic disturbances and apocalyptic or utopian futures, and perhaps one should, but I am intrigued by an idea floated by Steve Mentz in his notes towards a blue cultural studies: a much "less epic, more improvisational stories of working-with an intermittently hostile world." What would that song sound like?

New York, Oceanic City

Dean Kritikos

an ecological reading of megapolis

I. Premise
after Timothy Morton

A dam is Nature and
so is a damn
skyscraper.

The hues you
thought were Grey
are variations on a theme of Green

II. New York And/As the Ocean
after Jean-Paul Sartre

And Blue.

In 1945 my favorite philosopher
crosses the Atlantic to dive into a second sea—
visits my home town

Wherein he finds
he's all surrounded by
Nature, Nature crashing down
on him at every corner—

He reports to love New York after
getting over its "sickness, akin to sea
sickness"—it being so
unlike those European cities
Sartre is used to, "designed…
to conceal from [their inhabitants]
the inexorable presence of nature"[1]
   —to keep Nature out.
     New York has/is Nature, whether
     or not we want it. And that Nature isn't
     something separate from, up above, or
     down below the outright
     humanity, the anthropocentrism,
     of New York City:

  "All the hostility and cruelty of nature are present in
  this city, the most prodigious monument humanity
  has ever raised to itself. It is a light city; its apparent
  weightlessness surprises most Europeans. In this
  immense, malevolent space, this desert of rock that
  tolerates *no vegetation*, they have built thousands of
  houses out of brick, wood, or reinforced concrete,
  all of which seem about to fly away."[2]

1   Jean-Paul Sartre, *We Have Only This Life to Live: Selected Essays of Jean-Paul Sartre, 1939–1975*. Ed. Ronald Aronson and Adrian Van Den Hoven, eds. (New York: New York Review, 2013.) 119–25: 119.

2   Sartre, 123, my emphasis.

And how so? He also calls New York a jungle, probably
before the expression becomes a cliché, meaning that
he means it differently than you or I when we say "concrete
jungle"—it's less the concrete he's worried about,
      more the asphalt,
the avenues. New York is softer than you'd expect,
argues Sartre. Enter: Me: We need to think of New York
in terms of its fluidity rather than its hardness. It's
a "desert of rock," sure, but we might think of
any beach's sand the same way—rocks pulverized
from hardness not into oblivion but rather
a state more like the water
they segue into—each grain of sand,
like a drop of water,
nearly weightless in its own right.
You'll notice that "concrete"
is the last building material on his mind, coming up
after both brick
and wood. You'll know this:
that concrete is a liquid-turned-solid.
At the conclusion of his essay,
he'll talk about brick as "the color of dried blood,"
or another solidified liquid—the houses made of this Red
differ from European in age ("younger"),
but also in "fragility."[3] What's important
is that blood is operative as a liquid,
whereas concrete's function is solidity.

3   Sartre, 125.

He sees in New York the soft-ish stuff of the world,
the stuff of the city—not (set) concrete, but the stuff that
moves,
> and how "you move through it,"[4] as if swimming.
> No, "you don't go for a walk in New York."[5]
> "Moving through" a "city in motion" is partaking in its
> > action;
> there's no *ground* on which you might *walk*, no
> > ground
> against which you might be distinguished as a *figure*.
> > More on this later.
> What he's talking about is the Red, the Brown,
> > not the Grey—
The Black, which might be a darker shade—
> a burnt rendition—of Green—
which might be a Navy, might be a Blue:
> the asphalt-hue of avenues,
> > interrupted everywhere by Yellow, White.

> Asphalt is malleable, or at least moreso than concrete.
> Runners are supposed to plant their feet
> on the street instead of the sidewalk; the asphalt has
> > *give*,
> and won't *give* you bum knees as quickly as
> concrete will. A city of asphalt, an asphalt jungle,
> is a soft one, so

4   Sartre, 121.

5   Sartre, 121.

Unlike the "vertical city" Céline sees—a city Sartre
concedes New York to be, but only *after*
        it's a"lengthwise one."[6] He
privileges the avenues, the parallel "thoroughfares" of
        megalopolis.[7]
        Not the skyscrapers. Those are a fad.[8]
        The avenues, those soft and mobile
        expanses of space, are here to stay.
        He might have said *currents* instead, whether of
        water or wind:
            "I could find only atmospheres—
                        gaseous masses stretching out
                    longitudinally, with nothing to mark their
                                beginning or their end."[9]

                                —Morton's *mesh*, anyone?
        If, rather than "gaseous," Sartre had only evoked
                    the material of tennis shoes or
        basketball jerseys

        Or of orange juice. What is a city's boiling point?
        Gas might always be a literal degree away from
            liquid.

6   Sartre, 120.

7   Sartre, 120.

8   Sartre, 124–125.

9   Sartre, 121, my emphasis.

Because to Sartre, the city is a Nature that's not Green,
          but Blue—
or in-between—a Seafoam hue, a Tiffany box,
          an Aquamarine
that swallows you.

> "Am I lost in a city or in nature? New York affords
> no protection from the violence of nature. It is a
> city open to the skies. The storms flood its streets
> that are so wide and take so long to cross when it
> rains. The hurricanes, announced solemnly on the
> radio like the declarations of war, shake the brick
> houses and rock the skyscrapers. In summer, the
> air shimmers between the buildings. In winter, the
> city drowns as though you were in some Parisian
> suburb with the Seine overflowing, but here it is
> merely the snow melting."[10]

When's the worst and most literary time,
      the worst and most literary place,
      for a hurricane to strike?
              When we're sailing, of course,
                      on the open sea.
              Well, Jean-Paul, I'd say you're lost in both and neither,
              and, by your own logic, both lost and not:
              "You never get lost in New York"
          isn't undone by
              "I am never astray, but always lost."[11]

---

10   Sartre, 122.

11   Sartre, 122.

I come from a hard city that I want to soften, and
that city comes equipped with an even harder grid.
The lines are thick and straight on every map you
see—Gay Street is a famous little antithesis—and
seem to speak to causality.

"But there is no valid reason to justify my presence
at one spot rather than at another, since one place
is so like another," because
"the rigor of [New York's] defining coordinates,"
its "special precision…
is not accompanied by any emotional exactitude."[12]

Meaning
We might be talking about knots, naut miles.
Talking about and untying them, not cutting them in half.
Navigating in New York isn't a hard science—or it is,
at least as hard a science as the maritime arts seem
to someone who only drives a car. Or a science
that has to be *hard* because
its object is *soft* and *slippery*—the asphalt avenues
being velvety water not
only after it rains, but *before* it, too.
And *that* "is enough to soften somewhat the edges of the
harshest city in the world"[13]

12   Sartre, 122.

13   Sartre, 125.

III. Coastlines

Windows with warped glass make the sidewalk look like water
—Lee Ann Brown[14]

New York at first glance
looks designed to keep the ocean out:
we saw how well that worked with Sandy,
saw

the cup running over into
a second one—islands both vanishing
and appearing as the outer ocean decided
which parts of the inner one it wanted to reclaim;
I say that the land lost was not transubstantiated, though,
not changed in category.

The coast lines of New York
are an illusion: the ocean without
and the ocean within being continuous
rather than separate;

O'Hara reminds me that "one
need never leave the confines of New York
to get all the greenery one wishes"[15]

14   Brown, Lee Ann. "Warm and Fragrant Mangos, Thirty Calla
Lilies," *Out of This World: An Anthology of the St. Mark's Poetry Project,
1966–1991*, Anne Waldman, ed. (New York: Crown, 1991) 431.

15   Frank O'Hara, "Meditations in an Emergency," *The Collected Poems of
Frank O'Hara*, Donald Allen, ed. (Berkeley: University of California,
1995) 197.

—Blue too. The
shades of seafoam in-between
are what the greys
                allude to

So if we're all
of us plankton floating, or else
latched onto seats in
crowded buses, porous
trains, then where
is the boundary, the dam? Is
every damn skyscraper
a coral reef?—a
living thing
with biological significance
connected not just symbolically but
also symbiotically,
actually,
with
us humans and
any number of other creatures:

Cats mosquitoes cockroaches rats pigeons—
        pigeons being aquatic birds,
rats of sky and sea simultaneously, rats
                themselves being *of* the sea, *being* the sea—
                Like you and me in Metropolis, in Megalopolis, in
                Oceanopolis—in New York, Oceanic City.

Oceanic Valuation

Anne Harris

"**A** qui appartiendra ce briz?" screeches
Panurge as the tempest-tossed ship he clings to
heaves and groans towards becoming a wreck.[1]
To whom does a shipwreck belong? It belongs to the sea:
the word is a woeful concession to the mismatch between
oceanic power and human hopes and goods.[2] "Shipwreck"
belongs to its investors: it is also the word that activates
and justifies the claims of insurance, that human attempt to
negotiate (with) loss. Torn between possession and dispos-
session, the shipwreck manifests the struggle to account for
things.[3] Torn asunder, the shipwreck multiplies categories
of value. In asking about the reversals of fortune the ocean

1   François Rabelais, *Le Quart Livre de Pantagruel*, ed. Jean Plattard
     (Paris: Honoré Champion, 1910), esp. 93–105.

2   Steve Mentz, "God's Storms; Shipwreck and the Meanings of Ocean
     in Early Modern England and America," in *Shipwreck in Art and
     Literature from Antiquity to the Present Day*, ed. Carl Thompson
     (New York: Routledge, 2014), 77–91.

3   Larry Murphy, "Shipwrecks as Data Base for Human Behavioral
     Studies," in *Shipwreck Anthropology*, ed. Richard A. Gould
     (Albuquerque, NM: University of New Mexico Press, 1983), 65–89.

exacts in its shipwrecks, Panurge's question insists on the troublesome operations of oceanic valuation: the traumatic ways in which the ocean provokes humans to value things.

Ship/wreck

As the storm rages, Panurge compulsively begins to catalogue the parts of the ship straining apart. "The halyards have parted; our head-rope has shattered; our cable-rings have split asunder; the yard by the crow's nest is plunging into the sea; our keel is exposed to the heavens; our cables are nearly all broken."[4] The ship emerges in Panurge's panicked registry of parts, it comes into view through its fragmentation and splintering. Panurge will continue to name and value and mourn and scream throughout the duration of the storm. To the irritation of the rest of the crew, he does not act, he only accounts. In Rabelais's insistent drive of language, the panic of Panurge becomes a bad magic: as he names each thing, it falls to its destruction in the storm. Frère Jean desperately tries to shut him up, to shut down this nauseating naming-annihilating cadence. The ocean roils over the ship, the ship rolls beneath the ocean. Top(mast) is down(cast), "I can see neither sky nor Earth. Zalas, zalas! Of the four elements, all that's left to us here are fire and water." Panurge perseveres, his panic tumbling towards incoherence within the ship's disintegrating structure. The catalogue is soon broken up by the babbling of "Be be be: bouboubous bous bous:" language's helpless

---

4   François Rabelais, "The Fourth Book," from *Gargantua and Pantagruel*, trans. M. A. Screech (New York: Penguin Books, 2006), esp. 718–733.

effluvium before tragedy, its vapid awful mimicry of water's seepage into speech.[5]

Panurge is drowning, the ocean filling his mouth. But he resurfaces with one last request: "Just one little word to make my will, Frère Jean...Two words for my will and testament." Still counting and accounting, in what he believes to be his penultimate moment, he wishes to set down the ultimate value of his life. The ocean's yawning indifference hurtles him towards his own significance. But writing a will mid-gale is patently absurd, disparages Epistemon. A will only takes on value when its maker is dead and it survives. It is only if Panurge is separated from his will that it will do him any good, and its authorship at sea guarantees its demise rather than its execution. Epistemon tries to reason that action not accounting is required. Panurge counters with a romance of "some king's daughter, taking a pleasant stroll in the cool of the evening" happening upon his washed-up will. He dreams of his will perpetuating value beyond his life. The panic of Panurge displaces and misplaces value: from ship's part to language, from action to accounting. But in its hysterical swirling around value, it creates value, it instills the tragedy of loss, and it speaks

5   Or, Panurge is voicing a primordial noise, a return to the chaos
     of Genesis, to the becoming of multiplicity as it threatens unity,
     sounded out by Michel Serres, "[The ruckus] increases, it decreases,
     globally, locally it is multiple, various, variegated. Voices, cries,
     tears, thunderings, rumblings, whistles and crashes, breaths, blasts,
     grinding blows, chains and beats, cracklings and sounds, growling
     and waves, moans that die away...the river of noise carries along
     a thousand tonalities," *Genesis*, trans. Geneviève James and James
     Nielson (Ann Arbor: University of Michigan Press, 1995), 65. Panurge,
     in terror at the loss of his individual life, becomes part of the "river of
     noise" of the multiplicity of the ocean.

the fear the rest of the crew would deny in valorous action against the sea. It is when the storm abates that the pilot can call out a new catalogue of ship parts, this time as each is re-mastered by the crew, and that all are saved as land is sighted.

After all that panic, a calm. Panurge is revealed to be the fool: the object of Frère Jean's scorn, Pantagruel's frustration, and Epistemon's bewilderment for his constant decrying of the demise of every one and every thing. It is the fool that seeks to take account of things by making a count of things. And yet, Panurge was only doing (albeit with more rhetoric and flair) what maritime insurance was starting to develop: an accounting of value not only in terms of gain, but also in relation to potential loss.

Dry hopes

In a logic that begins with Roman maritime insurance, it is in estimating its loss that a thing's value is first revealed. Reversals of fortune at sea will go on to provoke a reversal of the early modern capitalist trajectory of value.[6] And so, in the age of nascent capitalism borne upon oceans, the valuation of a thing is fundamentally complicated: its potential gain in the marketplace is now intertwined with its potential loss at sea. Indeed, a thing's potential loss is its *primary* value: money for a good is paid into its insurance

---

6   Josiah Blackmore, "Manifest Perdition II: Going Under," from *Manifest Perdition: Shipwreck Narratives and the Disruption of Empire* (Minneapolis: University of Minneapolis Press, 2002), 89–107. "Two forms of currency—water and money—clash here, the former disempowering the latter," 99.

before it is paid into the marketplace.[7] Insurance seeks to
buoy dry hopes upon wet flows. It must carefully calculate
and balance both the optimism that goods will make it
to their destination, and the pessimism that they won't,
quantifying both the trust and mistrust of the sea. It takes
Panurge's panic and places its fervent accounting in a more
appropriate time and place: before the sea voyage, when
value can be calmly assessed and assured.

   In the same early modern period in which Rabelais'
neologisms and word plays jostled each other on the page,
maritime insurance was producing and aligning new
terminology that created new categories of value for things
after ocean storms. All of these terms, and their valuations,
become safeguards, attempts to put off or avoid relegating
things to that oldest word, the weariest tragedy: a wreck at
sea. "Lagan" was a word already in use, recorded as early as
1200, from a Scandinavian word family for things that lie
deep.[8] It is recorded again in 1531 to signify cargo that has
sunk and lies on the bottom of the ocean, but might yet
be reclaimed. Other terms of assessment have slipped out
of insurance language and into idiomatic speech. The pair
"flotsam" and "jetsam", both coined in the earliest years of
the seventeenth century, trace the physical trajectory of
things: flotsam floats upon the surface of the sea, awaiting
rescue and salvage; jetsam's fate, once it has been thrown
overboard to lighten the load of the ship, is unknown: it
will either become lagan, with a future rescue, or, another
new word: derelict, given up for lost at the bottom of the

---

7   James Franklin, "Aleatory Contracts: Insurance, Annuities, and Bets,"
    from *The Science of Conjecture; Evidence and Probability before Pascal*
    (Baltimore, MD: The Johns Hopkins UP, 2001), 258–288.

8   This and all etymologies are from the *Oxford English Dictionary*.

ocean.[9] A different set of values characterizes objects after a storm; the ocean appraises goods anew in their direct interaction with it. No longer held apart from the water by a ship, objects are revealed in various guises that are given language only in the age of capitalist commerce, when value begins to be projected well beyond the good itself.[10]

Medieval ship laws were fastened more tightly to the immediate material reality of goods in a storm. The Hamburg Ship Laws of 1301/6 and 1497 delineated an order of rescue: people, goods, and ropes.[11] The practice of "jettison" had no value beyond its action of throwing things overboard. It reveals the concerted effort of shipmen, however, that was perpetuated in other practices of shared risk. Before insurance articulated and quantified contracts and valuations, risk was shared in the principle of "averages," which distributed damages incurred during a sea journey.[12] Insurance further displaced the practice of

9   Skye Moody, "Flotsam's Noble Origins," from *Washed Up: the Curious Journeys of Flotsam and Jetsam* (Seattle, WA: Sasquatch Books, 2006), 15–75. Moody expands her exploration well beyond capitalist flotsam and jetsam to all manner of things that float or are projected by the sea: from ambergris to barnacles. She links Marx's "commodity fetish" to the practice of cargo cults (when objects washed ashore take on magical ore religious significance), 18.

10   Carl Thompson, "Shipwreck and the Forging of the Commercial Nation; the 1786 Wreck of the *Halsewell*," in *Shipwreck in Art and Literature from Antiquity to the Present Day*, ed. Carl Thompson (New York: Routledge, 2014), 92–111.

11   Edda Frankot, "Shipwreck, Jettison and Ship Collision in Maritime Law," from *'Of Laws of Ships and Shipmen': Medieval Maritime Law and Its Practice in Urban Northern Europe* (Edinburgh: Edinburgh UP, 2012), 27–52.

12   Frankot, 31–2. General average (for lost property), particular average (in case of accident), and petty average (tolls and customs) were all shared by those whose gains were most immediately involved with the voyage: merchants and ship owners. The term comes from the Arabic,

valuation: far from Panurge's panic in the midst of a storm, extrapolated from medieval pre-arranged agreements of action, insurance "decoupl[ed] the realm of values from the environment."[13] It disallowed total loss by attempting to displace and devalue the ocean's agency. Decisions about the value of objects were made in a time and place separate from the ocean's churning: before the journey, in board-rooms and assessors' offices. The ocean could then have its will, but the investors would have at least part of their way.

Wet flows

We have named this planet for what we can control of it. We till (the) Earth and invest its energies in ourselves. Unable to control the ocean, we hedge against it. The panic of Panurge and the displacement of insurance reveal the anxiety provoked by our loss of agency to what we have conceptualized through our fear to be the ocean's whim. Our attempts to understand the ocean have distanced our-selves from its churning as much as possible: older practices of navigation used the stars, celestial elements far removed from watery depths; insurance displaced the ocean's conse-quences from the loss of wreck to the salvage of accounting. Yet the ocean has movements of its own, which can draw us closer to it: not to control it, but to acknowledge the strange intimacy of its handling of our goods.

The ocean has been communicating itself to us through our goods for as long as objects have washed

awara and reflects the intersections of Christian and Muslim trade in the Mediterranean in the thirteenth century.

13 Cornel Zwierlein, "Renaissance Anthropologies of Security: Shipwreck, Barbary Fear and the Meaning of 'Insurance'," in *Humankinds: The Renaissance and its Anthropologies*, ed. Andreas Höfele and Stephan Laqué (Berlin: De Gruyter, 2011), 157–185.

up on shores. We are only now beginning to understand
how to read the ocean unto itself, how to understand its
movements, currents and gyres: what *it* values, where *it*
places its energies.[14] In doing so, we realize with more and
more accuracy, how much the character of the ocean—its
movement, its effect, its "whim"—is intertwined with that
of air. Ocean is as much wind as it is water.[15] In this new
understanding, Ocean is thus as much movement as it is
substance. And here is where our relationship to the ocean
is changing. If movement is a primal means of agency, the
ocean is an agent of exchange: it takes objects upon its
surface, keeps them in its depths, and relinquishes them
on "our" shores. It does this in the complex combination of
objects with its watery substance, its symbiosis with wind,
and the effect of time. Water and wind—what shapes the
ocean's currents, its movement—take tolls: they reconfigure
objects and revalue them.[16] They create new entities of
phenomenally divergent scale: from sea glass to the Great
Pacific Garbage Patch.

The journeys of flotsam all over the planet have
resulted in a field called "flotsametrics."[17] The combina-

---

14 The Perpetual Ocean project of the NASA Visualization Explorer
    reveals the flow and expanse of oceanic currents. http://svs.gsfc.nasa.
    gov/vis/a010000/a010800/a010841/index.html. With thanks to
    Steve Mentz for its reference.

15 Steve Mentz, "A Poetics of Nothing: Air in the Early Modern
    Imagination," *postmedieval* 4:1 (2013), 30–41.

16 Moody describes the organic flotsam of ambergris, which begins as
    a repugnant substance resulting from a whale's indigestion but, with
    the effects of water and wind over time, is transformed into a precious
    element of perfume and aphrodisiacs. "Dragon Spittle Fragrance,"
    28–39.

17 Curtis Ebbesmeyer and Eric Scigliano, *Flotsametrics and the Floating
    World: How One Man's Obsession with Runaway Sneakers and Rubber
    Ducks Revolutionized Ocean Science* (New York: Harper Collins, 2009).

tion of modern observational instruments and modern commercial goods has resulted in entirely new abilities to understand the ocean's movements. Spilled into the ocean by storms, our stubborn plastics create thick scars upon the ocean surface that are displaced by its currents. Curtis Ebbesmeyer and Eric Scigliano track the paths of commercial flotsam. Their primary materials are the goods of cargo containers washed overboard during storms that have unleashed millions of pairs of sneakers that wash then up on multiple shores. Boatloads of rubber ducks bob on the surface of the ocean to delicately, insistently, create a connect-the-dots of ocean patterns. The panic of Panurge absurdly materialized into a count that keeps coming; the displacement of insurance relegating bath toys to oceanic science. Flotsametrics has worked to further track the five major ocean gyres, including the North Pacific gyre holding our fascination along with the Great Pacific Garbage Patch. In revealing traceable paths and currents that can be named, our new science speaks of ocean's "memory" and of the "music of the gyres."[18]

The ocean is gathering our environmental degradation and denial unto itself. Perhaps Panurge, who saw his demise in the storm in terms of retribution, was not such a fool to panic. How to respond now? What would it be like to live in exchange with the ocean, to finally accept its formidable buoyancy as a fundamental condition rather than an accidental occurrence to insure against? How might we live within the ebb and flow of oceanic valuation?

18   Ebbesmeyer and Scigliano, 236–239.

Tourism, Experience, Knowledge, Action

Julie Orlemanski

For the better part of a decade, I've been a coast-dweller. I spent quite a few years in Boston, historied port city, and at the time of writing I live in Los Angeles, where my weekends are in darting back and forth across the Pacific Coast Highway, between mountains and surf. But this September [2014] I'll be moving to Chicago—a city, rumor has it, at some distance from the sea. Which is to say: I'm anticipating my imminent return to a primarily *touristic* mode of encountering the ocean. Soon enough, a week or two in the summertime will be my standard span for luxuriating in that oceanic feeling. But this is after all how I first encountered the Atlantic as a little girl: as vacationer and holidaymaker during annual family trips to one of the barrier islands along the North Carolina coast. Holden Beach was where, for me, the vast tidal swathe kept time on grey sands and the marshes flipped and shook their vivid grass. I was a passing visitor there, but the ocean covered a huge and permanent region of my girl-soul. All year, I would anticipate walking alone down the beach with my feet in the wavelets, telling myself new myths. And again: I was a passing and transient visitor

there, but it was within a permanent infrastructure that I
made my wide-eyed way: a mesh of supply-chains and util-
ities, bridge-buildings and dredgings, insurance schemes
and invasive species, condominiums and ice-cream parlors.
How does one measure the tourist's wonder against the
things that support it? What does the tourist come to know,
and what does she not?

The question I posed following the marvelous presentations at Oceanic New York had to do with tourism.
Beaches are tourist destinations *par excellence*—and so,
for that matter, is New York. To what insights, if any, are
sightseers and excursionists privy? What is the mode of
knowledge proper to vacations? The ways of knowing most
in evidence at Oceanic New York felt far from touristic.
Instead, dwelling's slower cadences characterized the
presentations, as did the sedimented, localized expertise
of habitation. Speakers attended to the historically tex-
tured intimacies of city and sea in the polluted waters of
Newtown Creek, the swells of the Hudson, and the tideline
strung with detritus along Dead Horse Beach. Memory and
urban history entwined. I was entranced by the speakers'
remarks, but I simultaneously had a growing sense of my
own difference. Over the course of the evening most of the
symposium-goers revealed themselves to be New Yorkers
of one stripe or another. They showed their localness
in small gestures of knowingness and intimacy, and in
this collectively conjured rapport, I became aware of the
specificity of my position. What did I feel? A wistful, easy-
breezy curiosity for a place I would shortly leave. I was
listening with the faintly envious, faintly careless comport-
ment of the visitor. It was this vague and dawning sense of
dissimilarity that gave rise to my question about tourism.
How, I suddenly wanted to know, do touristic ways of

understanding stand alongside those of the resident, the native, the inhabitant, the dweller?

If a fleeting impulse suggested my question, that impulse nonetheless arose from a longstanding preoccupation of mine. My sense is that the aesthetic and interpretive experiences of the kind that Oceanic New York set in motion are not fully dissociable from tourism. In fact, the humanities as a whole shares important homologies with tourism. What links them is the primacy of the category of *experience*, or the value placed on witnessing, proving on one's pulses, something's sensory and affective dimensions. How does the place where the land meets the sea *feel*? How do I react when it appears to me?—when it appears not necessarily immediately but within networks and frameworks of encounter, like the narratives and images that made up the symposium. If seaside tourism is often consumerist, depoliticized, parasitic, and environmentally destructive—it is also intimate, pleasurable, and (in some sense) revelatory. The humanities, arts, and tourism all center on experiential life, with its mingled aesthetic, affective, and ideational currents. All three can scale and mediate enormous entities—oceanic entities—for the human faculties of perception and thought. But they also leave things out. How do we evaluate the epistemology of experientially lush knowledge-objects?

My interest in heuristically aligning tourism with art and interpretation derives from an ongoing interest in how knowledge is experienced. Through what forms and figures do we come to know things? By which tropes, according to what models of data-visualization, do we discover? How is this knowledge then taken up into the practical dimensions of different persons' lives? I've often stumbled across such questions in the course of my scholarship and teaching.

Institutionally and pedagogically, I am called on to articulate what can be learned through close-reading and hermeneutic study. It is a matter not only of saying what we know and how we know—but also of explaining why this mode of knowledge has validity and value. Sociologically minded literary scholars have recently challenged literary history's experiential protocols. Franco Moretti in particular has made a series of provocative claims against the field-wide assumption that literary history depends on our reading (that is, experiencing) literary works. He argues that between the "pleasure and knowledge of literature" there is "no continuity"—"Knowing is not reading."[1] Moretti directs attention instead toward what close-reading obscures and excludes. At a minimum, arguments like Moretti's encourage us to be aware of the limitations of our experience of texts. But how does the reader learn the limits of her reading? How does a tourist find the limits of her experience, what subsists outside her awareness, making her pleasures possible?

Another occasion when I encountered versions of these questions—questions of how experience becomes knowledge, what kind of knowledge it is, and what good it does—took place during the Occupy movement. I was part of Occupy Boston and was writing for a fledgling progressive newspaper. As such, I was making and consuming, testing and reacting to representations both of the protests and of the inequalities in wealth and power that motivated them. Our group faced constant practical questions of communication: what rhetoric—what medium, tone, style, content, and form—suited what we wanted to say and do? How could we educate, persuade, and mobilize those who

---

1   Franco Moretti. "Moretti Responds." *The Valve: A Literary Organ*. Web. 12 Jan. 2006. www.thevalve.org.

watched or read? Rhetorical choices entail conceptions of how knowledge is experienced. The consequences of our implicit phenomenologies of communication were immediate. During the months we worked and wrote together, we struggled to negotiate the interchange between immense and complex entities, like global inequality, and reading, sensing, thinking individuals. Oceanic New York unfolded at a similar interchange, facing the vastness of the sea.

Matters of scale, experience, and contemporary rhetoric also implicate another topic, one that informed all of the conversations at Oceanic New York: climate change. What is to be done about global warming? No one's presentation took up the question directly, but it was asked again and again tacitly, especially as speakers reflected on Hurricane Sandy. A certain rudderless melancholy attended it. We all appeared to agree on the factuality of climate change, its imminence, and its dire consequences. Yet, given the facts and their urgency, why was effective change so far off? These unanswerables hovered like a cloud: is there something wrong with *how we know* and how we say what we know? Why isn't this knowledge turning into action? Marina Zurkow, who gave an excellent talk at Oceanic New York, also spoke the following day at BABEL's *Critical/Liberal/Arts* symposium, with Una Chaudhuri. Their presentation there staged the conundrum vividly. Zurkow and Chaudhuri shared images and sound-work from their collective art project on "inner climate change," which offered up new techniques for making climate change, that global catastrophe *non pareil*, personal, subjective, and felt.[2] Their documents set in motion (for me at least) a

2   See http://www.dearclimate.net/.

complicated reaction. At first, they seemed defeatist and quietist—for instance, with a series of posters about how to accommodate, rather than prevent, climate change. They were talking about how to survive rather than how to protest. Yet my resistance to the seeming complacency of "inner climate change" begged the broader question of alternatives. What were the strategies of subversion I would hold up as counterpoints? Weren't the outraged jeremiads and calamitous talking-points of those of us who accepted climate-change the same tactics that had shown themselves inadequate to stopping it? *Dear Climate*, as their project is titled, defamiliarized the interface between global warming and subjective life. It opened up different ways of conceiving the entrance of this massive and heterogeneous event into the everyday.

I have drifted far from the original theme of this essay, about how to value or devalue the mode of knowledge-production known as tourism, a mode that I suggested might not be so far from the experiential epistemologies of art and interpretation. The ultimate criterion I have been circling around is an instrumental one, namely the incitement to efficacious, beneficial action. Such a criterion leads away from the valuation of experience in itself and in the direction of an imperative, to make art and politics, aesthetics and praxis, the beautiful and the good meet and conjoin. Touristic experiences, no one is disputing, can be exquisite. The quality of my childhood touristic sensibilities, the delicacy of my wild girlish beachcomber's exaltation, was very fine—and the same is true for many people who come from near and far to spend their money and lug their beach-chairs down to the water and pitch their faces toward the blue-green horizon. But what of it? Pretty soon, the oceans will have swallowed our shores and cities.

This is a pessimistic little *essai* because its prediction, in the end, is that tourism will not turn out to be environmentally or politically salutary—which is another way of saying that the bond between an experience and the actions that would preserve the possibility of that experience is most uncertain, if not nil. And yet my hunch is that what I have not been able to think in my efforts to understand what mediates between each of us and the vast entities that demand our attention is the notion of the *collective*, or how those thinking, feeling individuals addressed by the category of experience might come together to act. A collective of tourists seems unlikely. But it is a nice vision, isn't it?—a fantasy of us droves of beach-goers, an army of vacationers, stepping out of the private rituals of our holidays, blinking, turning our heads left and right to peer along the strand. As we recognize the many crowded together, our numbers and our bathing-costume vulnerability and our closeness to the sea, perhaps then, in the sense of our being both here and in the conditions that brought us here, to the interface of the oceanic world, some gesture will stir the multitude of our bared limbs and a new shape of action overtake us, either dissolving us or preserving us where we stand.

Watery Metaphor

Jonathan Hsy

One of most compelling aspects of Oceanic New York was how its varied presentations aimed to explore and rethink metaphors of connectivity. The ocean is a conveyance-machine, a life-sustaining environment and agentive force in its own right, a dynamic medium/mode of transport that enacts the flow of matter, languages, and cultures. Emerging as another theme across the presentations was the idea that ocean invites us to adopt fluid modes of *temporality* as well. As I listened to the presentations, it became increasingly clear that thinking about the ocean requires a capacity to sustain different notions of scale concurrently. In a blog posting soon after the event Steve recalls "Nancy Nowacek's direct statement that we must live in more than one temporal register at the same time."[1] Indeed, these presentations moved into multitemporal registers through a variety of approaches: eco-theoretical, linguistic-poetic, philosophical-scientific, aesthetic-artistic, architectural-communal.

1 Steve Mentz, "Oceanic New York," http://stevementz.com/oceanic-new-york-2/. Posted October 2, 2013.

As Mentz observes, "There's no way to capture the fluid dynamism of the event itself—but formal play and poetic experiments can gesture toward that multiplicity in different media."[2] What I hope to offer in my response is a more deliberate consideration of the "fluid dynamism" of the event, exploring my current (pun intended?) thoughts on its multiplicity and play.

Linguistic Registers

A certain delight in wordplay and poetic experimentation with metaphor characterized many of the Oceanic New York presentations. In his etymological wordplay, Jeffrey Cohen evinces a transtemporal oceanic contact zone, and he does so in a writing style appropriate for relating the dispersal of peoples across time and thinking about the watery spaces they traverse.

Jeffrey's multitemporal experimentation with etymology and near-puns implying motion and polyglot vessels of transport ("convoy, convey, convoke") makes me ask how transportable different oceanic theories of connectivity become when they are expressed through poetic tropes (i.e., wordplay or metaphors). The transportability of oceanic paradigms (the question of whether a way of thinking about the ocean that derives from one context can carry over to another) is something that premodern scholars have contended with for some time. Indeed, it would appear that there is now a "critical mass" of different connectivity paradigms in play that are each to some

---

2   Steve Mentz, "Instructions for Oceanic New York," http://stevementz. com/instructions-for-oceanic-new-york/. Posted February 23, 2014.

Image 1: Oceanic New York, St. John's University, Sep. 26, 2013.
Eileen Joy, displaying her love of #disasterporn, shows an image
of a sublime green wave overtaking New York City.

extent unmoored from the specific oceanic spaces that generated them. I'm thinking of Sebastian Sobecki's work on South Pacific connectivity and its (admittedly cautious) application to a networked medieval Irish Sea and North Atlantic and Jeffrey Cohen's previous work, where archipelagic modes of thought migrate from the Caribbean to the British Isles; or explorations of connectivity informing the British archipelago to emerge in a forthcoming issue of *postmedieval*.[3] Very recently, Suzanne Conklin Akbari and Karla Mallette's wonderful co-edited collection *A Sea of Languages: Rethinking the Arabic Role in Medieval Literary History* has helped Anglophone readers to revisit connectivity via the profoundly intertwined literary his-

---

3   Sebastian Sobecki, *The Sea and Medieval English Literature*, (Cambridge: D. S. Brewer, 2008): 14–15; Jeffrey Jerome Cohen, *Cultural Diversity in the British Middle Ages: Archipelago, Island, England* (New York: Macmillan, 2008). A special issue of *postmedieval* edited by Sebastian Sobecki and Matthew Boyd Goldie will appear in 2016.

tories of languages and cultures throughout the medieval
Mediterranean.[4]

Akbari engages with recent work by David Abulafia on
the *longue durée* history of the Mediterranean and Horden
and Purcell's seminal *The Corrupting Sea* (among others)
to break out of constraining monolingual approaches to
literary history; she finds in the medieval past a more
expansive mode of (re-)de-territorializing discrete
linguistic, literary, and national traditions.[5] Most importantly for this discussion, Akbari also entertains how theories of connectivity that derive from this *particular* sea's
"enclosed" quality and movement of currents might actually
transfer to *other* landed medieval "Mediterraneans"—such
as the vast Sahara, or diverse terrain of the Silk Road (4). If
there is a single global ocean then an "Oceanic New York"
just happens to be one locality among many in a contigu-
ous terraqueous globe.[6] Rather than perpetuating a rigid
distinction between land and sea, "both/and" orientations
take connectivity as a feature traversing all spaces (a point I
suggest in a *different* way in my own work).[7]

4   Suzanne Conklin Akbari and Karla Mallett, *A Sea of Languages:
    Rethinking the Arabic Role in Medieval Literary History* (Toronto:
    University of Toronto Press, 2013).

5   David Abulafia, *The Great Sea: A Human History of the Mediterranean*,
    (Oxford: Oxford University Press, 2011); Peregrine Horden and
    Nicholas Purcell, *The Corrupting Sea: A Study of Mediterranean History*,
    (London: Wiley-Blackwell, 2000).

6   See the "Oceanic Studies" cluster in *PMLA* 125:3 (2010): 657–735,
    edited by Patricia Yaeger, and also Steve Mentz, "Toward a Blue
    Cultural Studies: The Sea, Maritime Culture, and Early Modern
    English Literature," *Literature Compass* 6/5 (2009): 997–1013.

7   Jonathan Hsy, *Trading Tongues: Merchants, Multilingualism, and
    Medieval Literature* (Columbus: Ohio State University Press, 2013).

YOU ARE STANDING WHERE A THREE ACRE GLACIAL POND ONCE STOOD. IT WAS CREATED BY A MILE HIGH GLACIER DURING THE LAST GREAT ICE AGE 18,000 YEARS AGO. THE GLACIER LEFT HUGE BOULDERS THAT IT CARRIED AND DEPOSITED THUS CREATING THE TERMINAL MORAINE: "THE BACKBONE" OF LONG ISLAND. IN 1907, A 100 ACRE GOLF COURSE WAS BUILT NEAR THE POND FOR JAMAICA ESTATES AND IS NOW THE HOME OF ST. JOHN'S UNIVERSITY.

ONCE CALLED "REDDER'S POND", IN 1931 THE CONSTRUCTION OF THE GRAND CENTRAL CAUSED THE POND TO BE DRAINED AND COVERED OVER BY MUCH OF THE PARKWAY.

ERECTED BY:
THE AQUINAS HONOR SOCIETY
IMMACULATE CONCEPTION SCHOOL
ST. JOHN'S UNIVERSITY

Image 2: Stone marks former site of glacial pond.
St. John's University, Sep. 26, 2013.

Watery Motion

In *A Sea of Languages*, Karla Mallette pinpoints an excellent
linguistic metaphor to suggest new ways of thinking across
different scales of time concurrently. In "Boustrephedon:
Toward a Literary Theory of the Mediterranean," Mallette
puts Classical writing and reading practices in conversation
with the medieval Mediterranean Sea for the benefit of
modern-day readers. "Boustrophedon," she notes, is a
Greek adverb denoting "turning as the ox plows," and
insofar as the adverb denotes motion it provides a
model for conceiving the back-and-forth transit of texts,
languages, and ideas. As Mallette states, a "tidal rhythm of
ebb and flow" implicates "our contemporary entanglement
with the Arab world to the medieval Mediterranean," a
globe where Arab and European worlds implicate one
another (260). This back-and-forth mode of thought
registers—however unexpectedly—with Lowell Duckert's
presentation on "glacial erratics" and the flow of ice, and
the Iroquois name for the Hudson (entity of water) as the
"river that flows both ways."

I love what these models of back-and-forth transit
achieve and would add that the *materiality* of the
"boustrophedon" metaphor warrants further consideration,
as it weirdly enacts an amphibious leap across land to
water. That is, "boustrophedon" originally refers to the
motion of a yoked ox in a profoundly landed, agricultural
context—and it is being extended *by analogy* to a sea and
the fluid modes of conveyance it enables. The landedness of
the "boustrophedon" metaphor renders it simultaneously
alien to and appropriate for limning the surfaces of an
enclosed sea.

As we test the flexibility of oceanic metaphors to
structure thought, we are eventually faced with Hester

Blum's dictum: "The sea is not a metaphor."[8] Or rather (as Steve suggested in his presentation) the sea is *not only* a metaphor. Adopting a spatial metaphor that thinks not in terms of back-and-forth surface motion but plumbs the ocean's watery depths, Blum observes: "Oceanic studies calls for a reorientation of critical perception, one that rhymes with the kind of perspectival and methodological shifts…seen [in] influential conception[s] of history from the bottom up" (671). In this shift to a vertical/horizontal orientation, Blum cannot help but wax poetic with a metaphor of her own: the conceit that one critical orientation "rhymes" with another.

Waves (Sound and Water)

Blum's use of "rhyme" to indicate critical orientations that resemble one another brings me ultimately to one physical, kinetic feature of the ocean: waves. And here I mean waves of water and of sound. Many of the essays in this volume employ rhetorical features to suggest the materiality of oceanic metaphors and watery poetics. Wordplay and the poetic effects of cadence and rhyme not only help transmit to ideas but they also implicate sound as a key mode of idea-conveyance. Sound, to adopt modern scientific discourse, is a vibration that propels itself as waves through a fluid medium (be it water or air). It might not be surprising, then, that we can resort to stylized patterning of sound-waves to convey how we—terrestrial, air-breathing creatures—conceive transit through a water-filled environment. To communicate some sense of transit through waves and currents of water, we create verbal and linguistic

8   Hester Blum, "The Prospect of Oceanic Studies," *PMLA* 125:3 (2010): 670.

Image 3: Moments in time.
Spencer Finch's *The River That Flows Both Ways* (2009) documents
a single day's journey along the Hudson through snippets of color.
Finch photographed the changing colors of the Hudson once every minute.
This combination of two photos was taken at the High Line on Sep. 28, 2013.

"waves" (in medieval acoustic theory, sound breaking air)
to enact analogous motion. As Patricia Yaeger observes, a
contemporary "rush of aqueous metaphors [across oceanic
studies] lends materiality to a world that becomes more
ethereal every day, to a discourse that has taken to the air,
that threats iPhones like oxygen saps, as if our very lungs
and sinews could be extruded into cyberspace."[9] I might
tweak this observation slightly to say that attending to the
materiality of metaphor *and sound* exposes how the ocean
facilitates thought in a global (literary, linguistic, temporal)
scale.

9   Patricia Yaeger, "Editor's Column: Sea Trash, Dark Pools, and the
     Tragedy of the Commons," *PMLA* 125:3 (2010): 523.

Oceanic New York has helped me to think more carefully about materiality of metaphor, or—to put it another way—to confront the physicality of thought. Sonic patterns and verbal tropes are one strategy for making ideas perceptible to the senses, so it is fitting that thinking about the ocean and diverse watery environments would provoke such varied concurrent modes of expression. These presentations in the original "event" of their oral-aural-sonic delivery and in their printed manifestation in graphic form cover a range of topics, but collectively they achieve a shared effect: they seek to embody varied modes of transit through space and time. Such embodied linguistic mimicry is not limited to sound: H-Dirksen Bauman's work on Deaf literary theory notes the American Sign Language gesture for the verb FLOW manually enacts a downward motion resembling water, enacting a "kinetic model of the world."[10]

These acts of watery thinking in all their variety instill an attentiveness to the terraqueous worlds we inhabit. These concurrent critical modes—and ludic exploration of metaphor and language—reveal the manifold functions of the ocean and attend to the perpetual motion of all that participates in it, with it, and through it. The essays in this collection, however varied in scale and scope, collectively enact the grand connectivity of time and space of oceanic metaphor while also engaging with the ocean's dynamic material reality.

10 H-Dirksen Bauman, "On the Disconstruction of (Sign) Language in the Western Tradition: A Deaf Reading of Plato's *Cratylus*," *Open Your Eyes: Deaf Studies Talking*, ed. H-Dirksen Bauman (University of Minnesota Press, 2008), 127–145: 141.

Building a Bridge by Hand to Cross Buttermilk Channel on Foot

Nancy Nowacek

August 19, 1900

W alt Whitman reports the *Barbarossa's* passage through Buttermilk Channel. It is a large German vessel with a draft of 28 feet. He writes an article for the *Brooklyn* titled, "It's really a Channel": "A few years ago moderate sized barks had an unhappy habit, in consort with their towboats, of going aground near the Atlantic Dock gap. There was much recrimination, a good deal of hard swearing, but there was no dispute that there was a [sand]bar in Buttermilk Channel." Whitman provides an antecedent about the Channel's name: "the title of Buttermilk Channel is derived from the days of the Revolution when a two gun battery swept the upper bay. The colonists were not over blessed with wealth or food and the farmers drove their cows across the [sand]bar that then led to Governor's Island. When the cows missed the low tide they had to swim home and as a result their lacteal processes resulted in sour milk. Hence Buttermilk Channel."[1]

1   *Brooklyn Eagle*, Aug 19, 1900, 5. Accessed via http://eagle.brooklynpubliclibrary.org/Repository/getFiles. asp?Style=OliveXLib:LowLevelEntityToSaveGifMSIE_ BEAGLE&Type=text/html&Locale=english-skin-custom&Path=BEG/ 1900/08/19&ChunkNum=-1&ID=Ar00506

August 22, 2011

In studying the history of Buttermilk Channel and Governors Island, I discover the Whitman piece, and the fabled
sandbar.

March 22, 2012

I leave home at 6:30 A.M., take the B61 bus to Borough Hall,
and descend into multiple connecting hallways to find the
R train to Whitehall Street. I travel one stop. I board the
ferry at 7:30 with construction workers, engineers, high
school teachers on bikes with thermoses of coffee, high
school students in backpacks and baseball hats in the
waiting room at the ferry terminal. The ferry docks on
the northern pier of Governors Island. We disembark and
climb upwards into the island. I move into my temporary
studio on the island, and from that point on, I tell fellow
artists, friends, professional colleagues, and any stranger
who will listen, "I am building a bridge to Governors Island."

April 14, 2012

At 8:12 A.M., I ascend from the Whitehall station out into
lowest Manhattan, walking against the waves of morning
commuters swelling northward out of the Staten Island
Ferry terminal. Picking my way through them, I board
a nearly empty return boat. It is a slow trip, as the vessel
lumbers and rolls through the harbor. Panicked for time
and disoriented by the protocols of Staten Island, I find
myself in a cab with a Mental Health worker, sharing a trip
across the island to the US Coast Guard's Headquarters,
and then the Mental Health facility. I am 30 minutes late,
making apologetic phone calls to my host.

I lay down sketches of boats strung together, bamboo rafts lined with people, beach rafts sewn together and housed in a PVC pipe frame. The heads of Waterways Management, Marine Event Permitting (fireworks! Fleet Week!), and the Waterways Management Coordinator sit respectfully and gaze over them in silence as I stumble through my idea and my list of questions.

They offer the distant possibility that there *could* be some consideration of a future day where Buttermilk Channel (a major International Shipping thoroughfare) *could* be closed to boat traffic for a temporary floating pedestrian bridge. To be permitted as a Marine Event, Waterways Management would need to enter the event into the public record and allow 180 days for discussion. The clock is ticking: if I can create a workable design in 3 weeks' time, I stand a chance of getting permission to install the project in late August 2012.

A month later, I am no closer to a workable design, and have learned just enough to know that this project will take years longer than the six months I'd hoped.

June 4, 2012

The second apartment buzzer sounds at 5:05 A.M. It is the videographer. Once we review the details, the actor climbs into the cow costume, and we are off. Re-enacting Whitman's tale of farmers walking their cows to graze on the island, our modern version requires a quarter-mile walk to the F train, stairs, turnstiles, escalators to an R train, more stairs, more turnstiles, and several more blocks to a 6:30 A.M. ferry. In total, what should be a five-minute walk across a sandbar takes us 78 minutes.

June 15, 2012

I receive an apologetic call from my contact at the Coast Guard: "I'm so sorry to say that it seems your bridge…is really a bridge." She continues on to explain that I need to speak to the Bridge Branch division because, now that the project is on its radar, the division will require me to complete a bridge permit application. Her tone suggests an insurmountable challenge and an end to the project.

I phone the head of the Bridge Branch Division. He explains to me that my project fulfills the USCG's basic definition of a bridge: "Any structure that crosses a channel to transport goods, people, etc, in the USCG's eyes is a bridge; and even if temporary, every bridge must go through a nine-month (if not longer) review process, including public notice procedures…Bridges are, at their core, obstructions to marine navigation. The reason that boats put up with them is that they permit other kinds of transport to occur."

July 28 2012

After dozens of emails, false starts and weather cancellations, I final have a chance, with the Village Community Boathouse to join a rowing expedition in Buttermilk Channel. It is a cool grey morning. We meet at the navy yard, load an eight-man, 26-foot Whitehall gig into the water, and follow with safety vests and paddles. The launch is smooth, but once we enter Buttermilk Channel, everything changes. Although we are rowing with the current, it is some of the hardest physical work I have ever done. Every part of me is sweaty.

I think to myself, *This is the hard part*, until a 100-ft. barge barrels through on the shoulders of a tug. We are set into violent, unpredictable rolling by its wake. From that point on, every part of me is tense, and sweaty, and certain we are going to capsize. I think to myself, *But I love the water*, and myself answers, *This is not the water, this is a watery superhighway*.

I have never been so happy to see land as when we heave towards Valentino Pier. The boat feels unmovable as we drag it through the shallow tide onto shore. I am so grateful for the experience, and even more grateful that I will not have to continue on to Pier 40 in the Hudson. I hate that I am afraid of the water. My fear underscores the need for the bridge. I continue forward.

October 6, 2012

Three of us carry Citizen Bridge 1.0 to the shore at Valentino Pier. As soon as its PVC railing is rebuilt and ratchet straps tightened, two of us move it into the surf,. We drag it out to a few feet's depth, and it begins bobbing with greater force. As I stabilize it, a friend attempts to mount the deck in order to stand. Before he can get a second knee on, a wave rises and flips both him and the piece over into the water, splintering the model into a dozen pieces. Version 1.0 lasted little more than three minutes, More R&D is needed, as well as consulting the tide tables before future tests.

Three weeks later, Hurricane Sandy strikes the city, shifting the waterfront's focus to recovery. Red Hook is devastated, and we all spend as much time as we can before night hits helping the neighborhood to clean up and rebuild.

February–April 2013

I pursue meetings with all necessary agencies involved in the bridge permit application. Via phone calls and conference tables, I meet with the head of the Bridge Division to review in detail the requirements of the 42-page bridge permit application manual, the US Army Corps of Engineers, the Mayor's Office for Environmental Coordination, the Department of Environmental Conservation, the Port Authority via the manager of the Brooklyn Cruise Terminal, the head of waterfront development for the NYC EDC, the director of the Trust for Governors Island, and the director of waterfront development for the NYC Planning department.

Each of those agencies requires a permit, and all those permits are required as part of the Bridge Permit Application. After reviewing the requirements, it is abundantly clear that in order to complete any of the permits, a final workable design is necessary. So back to the drawing boards.

June 26, 2013

Citizen Bridge 2.0 launches! With the support of a residency from Recess, a non-profits art space in SoHo and their partnership with Pioneer Works in Brooklyn, we— myself and three recent architecture graduates from Pratt Institute—have spent six weeks discussing, designing and building this second design.

Citizen Bridge 1.0 was 4'×3' of decking affixed to a piece of chain-link fence gate and a pair of 30 gallon drums, weighing 30 pounds. Version 2.0 was constructed of 4×8 sheets of ¾″ plywood, 2×4s, threaded steel rods and 55 gallon drums. Each unit of version 2.0 weighs approximately 300–400 pounds. A team of eight men of super-human strength and a scissor lift were necessary to move each piece from their second-floor build location to the street.

Launch day. Sixteen volunteers—good friends and strangers too curious to remain bystanders—roll the pieces over cobbled and pock-marked streets to Valentino Pier. Despite my years of summers at the pier, the low fence around the park's perimeter never registered. It takes all of us to lift each piece over the fence and over the rocky ground to the water.

In the surf, we are joined by an expert kayaker who helps direct the process as Brady (lead architect) and I drag the pieces towards one another to join them. It's a hot day and the the coolness of the water—despite my fears of its bacteria content—feels rejuvenating. As we drag the two lumbering units further out, I am directed—with great urgency—to move from in-between the two pieces so that I don't get crushed as they roll with the surf.

Once the pieces are joined, it's an easy hoist myself onto the structure—like getting out of the deep end of a pool. The bridge piece is big and heavy and takes the waves like a Cadillac. It's exhilarating to stand astride the join. Four others join me atop of the prototype. It is a triumphant moment. We are one step closer to reality.

Having taken on considerable water during the launch, each piece now weighs pver 400 pounds. They are formidable loads to walk from the shore to the edge of the park, and lift back over the fence to be rolled back through the streets. Too big, too heavy, too cumbersome: to build one hundred seventy-five of these an illogical path.

November 16, 2013

The wood has been delivered from the lumber yard on the Gowanus, and the barrels from the container warehouse in Bushwick. We assemble at 10 A.M. on Pier 40 at the Village Community Boathouse. Two architects, a journalism professor-slash-boat-builder, and professor of game design-slash-former-skate-ramp-builder. We have come together to build Citizen Bridge 3.0.

We assemble three frames from 2×4s, attach plywood decks, and fasten them to pairs of drums with ratchet straps. We discuss the pros and cons of decking made from furring strips versus plywood sheets, and at my insistence, we try one of each for comparison. We build a preliminary railing system, affixing it to the middle of the three modules. Once the modules are joined, the grouping is rigged with line, lifted by the pier's electric gantry, and lowered into the river 15 feet below. We don safety vests, and one by one, pick our way over the edge, down a rusty ladder onto the structure. The scale of the pier, the Hudson River, and the city skyline in the distance dwarf Citizens Bridge 3.0. It feels more like a Huck Finn raft than a bridge.

Faster, lighter, cheaper: 3.0 feels like a great step forward in construction but half a step back in sturdiness.

December 18, 2014

At the invitation of Captain John Doswell, Maritime producer, president of the Working Harbor Committee, member emeritus of the Hudson River Park Trust, and lead advisor to Citizen Bridge, I am drinking a beer in a bar on the edge of South Street Seaport to celebrate the holiday season with the Metropolitan Waterfront Alliance. John introduces me to the former Executive Director of the Port Authority, the former Chief Operating Officer for Battery Park City, and Vice President of the Hudson River Park. Doswell is most connected and (in my estimations) the most beloved figure on the waterfront. Through him I've also met the former Executive Director of the Port Authority, the former CEO of the Circle Line, the Waterfront VP of the EDC, the owner of NYC Water Taxi, members of the Army Corps, the Sandy Hook Pilots, boat owners, boat captains, helicopter pilots, waterfront advocates, and many others who describe themselves as having salt water in their veins.

December 31, 2013

Before his retirement on January 3, 2014, the head of the USCG Bridge Branch Division offers to ignite the permitting process by circulating our proposal through the region. On New Year's Eve, I send him a letter outlining the project definition (a demonstration project), vision, needs it fulfills, as well as all developments to date. I send an identical letter to the head of the Trust for Governors Island.

February 1, 2014

I am laid off from my research position. Now unemployed, there is even more time to pursue the bridge.

February 12, 2014

John Doswell and I meet inside the Staten Island Ferry Terminal. He has been allowed by the Harbor Operations Steering Committee to accompany me to present Citizen

Bridge to what I come to learn is essentially the Harbor's League of Justice. We are escorted through an unmarked door, an elevator, and hallways to a conference room hidden in the top corner of the Staten Island Ferry building. There are over twenty people in the room. It is a respectful but tough crowd. After my presentation and discussion, the committee makes no ruling, but offers a series of advised next steps in order to further develop and define the project at greater level of detail.

Februrary 28, 2014

I am sitting in a conference room looking out over Brooklyn Bridge Park across a conference table from two leaders of the Brooklyn Bridge Park. After presenting the basics of the project with a request to situate a test model in the waters between their piers, they are warm, enthusiastic, and fully understand the mission and logic behind the project. Another relationship is born, another bridge built.

March 4, 2014

The 8:35 LIRR to Glen Cove is quieter than I'd imagined. At the advice of the Steering Committee, I am traveling to the nation's premiere college for naval architecture and engineering, the Webb Institute, to present Citizen Bridge to its student body and faculty. The Institute is situated on the Long Island Sound in a traditional English Country Manor from the late nineteenth century. It's a beautiful place, filled with model ships of all size and type. The students are incredibly knowledgeable and excited. They fire a round of sophisticated questions my way, and a relationship is born.

April 2, 2014

To my confusion, the driver from the lumber yard pulls up
to the sidewalk of the loading dock of my studio building
in DUMBO, but not up to the loading dock. "Truck won't
fit." As he unbuckles the tie-downs around my wood, he
continues, "delivery means 'to the loading dock'. Hope you
got someone to help you." He drops each 75-lb. piece of
plywood on the dock, several feet from the freight elevator.
And then he dumps the dozens of 2×4s.

I don't have anyone to help me.

April 4, 2014

With all the wood and barrels necessary, we—young architect, game design professor and I—begin building Citizen
Bridge 3.1. The public has been invited to our studios so we
are building another version of the November prototype.
Within the first hour, our muscle memory kicks in and
we move quickly assembling barrels to platforms with
strapping. It takes several unplanned hours to improvise a
first-generation railing system, an omission in past versions.
The railing is completed with a prototype name plaque system to represent those who have contributed to the project.

June 6, 2014

In the past three months, Glen Cove transformed into a
paradise on Long Island Sound. A dozen Webb Institute
students and faculty have assembled to workshop Citizen
Bridge 3.1. After briefing the students on the constraints
and design of the project, they begin work. Some are
writing equations, others are making sketches. At one point,

there is a question: "Does it have to be eight feet wide or could it be four feet?" As we unpack the implications, it's clear that we're on to another design revision.

July 11, 2014

After navigating from south Brooklyn from one traffic jam to another, we queue up the U-Haul at the base of Manhattan behind cement trucks and an ice cream truck. Fully loaded with 12 barrels, plywood, three dozen 2×4s, power tools, bagels and sandwiches, we are eventually waved on to the ferry to begin building Citizen Bridge 4.0 on Colonel's Row to display at City of Water Day. As we build on the lawn, the city watches our progress from the north. The harbor is ecstatic with sailboats, taxis, ferries, tugs, and barges on this dazzling summer day.

This prototype bears uncanny resemblance to one of the first renderings in 2012, and in this way the process has come full circle. To advance, we need experienced engineers and designers to join us.

Over the past two years, Citizen Bridge has become not just a bridge but a network: experts and amateurs, coming together to fulfill a vision about reclaiming public access to the waterfront and reimagining the ways in which the water is public space. It's not just about walking across a channel. Citizen Bridge aims to demonstrate to the power structures that govern our waterways new potential to collaborate in the forging of a public waterfront committed to reciprocity between a city, its commerce, and its people.

As a temporary installation, Citizen Bridge is an attempt to focus attention and amplify the harbor's opportunities as a living, working public resource and space. Citizen Bridge aims to activate public interest from the Bronx to the Battery, Newtown Creek and Red Hook to Sunset Park and the Verrezano, and beyond. Together, we will reinstate the power of citizens to engage the built environment, returning to the idea that urban space is the aggregate of such actions, and that cities are constructed by acts of imagination.

Oceanic Dispatches

Jeffrey Jerome Cohen and Allan Mitchell

Image 1: Shell.

Dear A,

I **am landlocked** and dreaming of the sea.
Born near the coast, companioned by storms and swells, I've grown weary of summer thundershowers, puddles, brooks that purl, the mud under gutters, water without brine. I miss the ocean's tang, touch and din. The Atlantic has a language even cloudbursts cannot translate. Not knowing how else to capture something marine, this

morning I added sea salt to a milk glass and filled it from the tap. Into my kitchen sea I dropped a stone and scallop shell. Speckled granite plaything of the waves, the rock is round like an egg. I am guessing that breakers rolled it longer than Maine's shores have known human trace. The shell is much younger, and in a few years would have been sand. Both are stones, really: it's just that one shows its creatureliness better. Both are intimates of pelagic tang, touch and din. I enclose with this message a dry picture. It conveys little of sense.

I've fucked up, I know. The sea is a force, not drops for glassware. Oceans cannot be domesticated, cannot become small. There's no life in my inland sea, no crash or tumult. Without my hand nothing moves. Its water came from a river swiftly making for a bay. I interrupted a seaward course and housebound an element.

But I keep thinking that the glass is made of melted sand. The O of its rim initiates *Okeanos*, the embracing world sea, that marine ouroboros. The water the tumbler held has already vanished through the drain, is already headed for Potomac and Chesapeake, flowing towards estuary, salt expanse, dispersion, droplets perhaps for future hurricanes. This O, this ocean-word or ocean-ward, is vast, even in a milk glass: transport as well as fragment of an inhuman language.

I wonder if you would write to me, as you think about vast oceans, a story of the sea.

Respectfully yours,

J.

Dear J,

Your experiment seems to have brought
you to the edge, though nowhere more lunatic than
the ocean itself. Let me try to identify the source of
this maniacal thought I have. Even this may amount to no
more than an amusing folly.

I grew up in a pacific seaside city on a so-called Half
Moon Bay, one of many strewn along these western shores,
upon which is inscribed the deep sympathy of astronomi-
cal and aquatic elements. Up and down the coastline long
crescent beaches are impressed with the gravity of the situation, geographic testament to the way otherwise discrete
bodies crisscross one other, like the swash and backwash of
waves sculpting the shore. Plutarch rehearsed the old line
that the moon's face is a mirror reflecting fleeting images
of ocean (earthshine denotes the phenomenon today), but
the moon seems to generate rather more enduring earthen
images of its phases. Raising the tides, the moon effectively
renders coastland lunulate.

Play with stone and seawater then. Are we not caught
between those twin forces anyway? I harbor a crazy sus-
picion that we are in fact surrounded, and that there is no
escaping the influences that (also, yes) elude capture. All
our briny bodies are surely subject to the virtual pull, no
matter how far removed.

Ancient and medieval writers at least claim that the
human—*moncynne* according to the punning fourth
Exeter Riddle—is touched by the moon. All moonstruck.
To one with monocular vision doubtless everything can
seem oceanic. There is no vessel too small to register the
monthly flux. Menstruum or moisture in the brain, for

instance. Pliny thought our blood too ebbs and flows according to the phases of the moon. Your shell, he would have said, grew thanks to the power of the rocky overhead satellite. The moon is likewise supposed to be a distant cause of the generation of infants, newly grafted trees, seeds, honey, fish, and fowl.

It would be loony to think everything conspired against our loneliness. All I know is that I've never been able to move far from the sea, having started out playing in sand and surf before coming to make a home, surrounded even now, on an island in the Pacific.

A.

~~~~~~~~~~~~~~~~~~~~~~~~~~~~~~

Dear A,

My sleep is restless when the moon is round—troubled dreams, perhaps, or longing for the sea. Strange to feel such pull from dust. But you are right: other ages had a better vocabulary for celestial gravity, for the lunacy that pulls at oceans and blood. Gerald of Wales, dreaming of an island to conquer, wrote that as the moon waxes the seas swell, the vital fluids of every living creature surge, the sap that is the life of plants rises. All things are ruled by the moon, all things are lunatic, all things are full of roily ocean. Medieval words that arrive when I think of the Atlantic and the moon's traction: *lunaticus, lunage, lunatique, lunetie, lunatyke.*

I write this letter from the coast of Maine, in the December clarity of what I am told is called the "Cold" or "Long Night" Moon. My father's family has lived here since the 1880s, when they fled European pogrom. I have been thinking therefore about convoys: the groups we form with others, united for a while in journeys, safety against elements. A convoy is odd fellowship, like and unlike, humans with objects, oceans as roads, machine for strange cargos, and also stowaways. If the sea is a conveyance device, if metaphor is a machine of transport, then through convoys we join with others in the hope of destination. Tempests, pirates, monsters of the depths, rogue waves, icebergs and icelock are the things of encounter that keep wanting to become allegories, but I think we should let them speak in their own tongues.

Sea is a space of story. Our letters are proof enough of that. But I've been wondering what happens when narrative becomes waterlogged, when brine stain or rainsoak wipe words from the page. Isn't that what happened to *Beowulf*, when a flood quenched the dragon transition and took some words of the poem to oblivion? Funny to think these letters—these ones now, the ones I am writing on the Atlantic coast, snow at the waves, and yours from that other ocean—these words will last the fifty years of electronic media, and perhaps twice that in paper form. Had they been inscribed on flayed sheep they might have attained the millennium. Skin as conveyance device, death the price for story's endurance. Or maybe rain or the sea would have taken the words all the same, and maybe the ocean swallows more than conveys.

These words are written late at night under lunar radiance in a place of family where, in days to come, we will not be known. I'd send them to you with sand, or with some trace of sea, but I do not think this cold Atlantic can know what happens at your coast. Your Half Moon Bays (how I envy them) seem calm and deep, your lives not so stormy.

Tide means time. What unforgivable redundancy to cliché those words together, time *and* tide. Oceans convey rhythmically, ebb and flow, catastrophe and flourishing, lunatic cyclicality. These words, no matter how oceanic, will not endure.

J.

P.S. I enclose for your enjoyment a lunar postcard, from the moon-struck Isidore, who heard in words the noisy materiality of the things they named. The moon, he thought, takes its name [*luna*] from solar radiance [*lux*]. But he admitted that sometimes lunar intensity renders people *lunaticus*, making them believe inhuman forces impress themselves on bodies like moonlight.

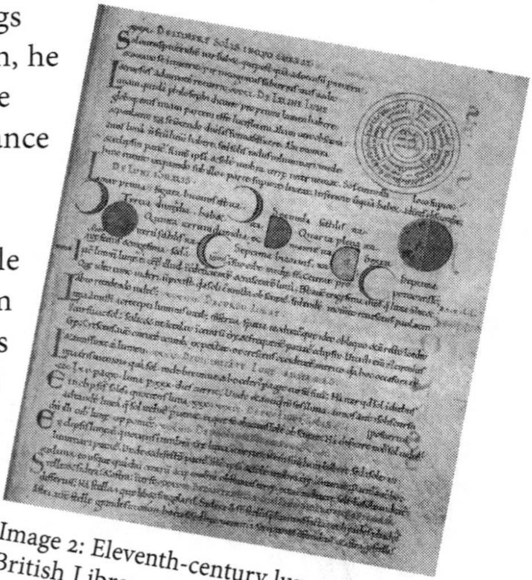

Image 2: Eleventh-century lunar postcard. British Library, Royal MS 6.C.i, f. 30ʳ.

Dear J,

A storied sea transports us, and yet as you also observe, sea stories are not all ours to tell. I too strain to hear things outside speak as if "in their own tongues." You and I are moved to correspond over immense distances nonetheless, exchanging these letters as if mere words could navigate the passages.

Am I falling prey to a little allegory? Inevitably so perhaps, but let me start here in the hopes of ending up elsewhere.

Some will insist that aquatic allegories are poor human contrivances, fabricated accounts that correspond to nothing external. So I have been thinking lately of the way Hesiod for one depicts the moon-goddess Selene, "having bathed her lovely body in the waters of the Ocean," newly cleansed and clarified by the so-called monthly ablution. An oceanic event is transformed into hydromythic hymnody. Has an encounter between moon and earth been displaced and domesticated in the process? What remains of orbiting celestial bodies, moonshine, and brine? I'm just mad enough to think some more-than-human influence comes streaming through, and cling to the thought that a poet's verses convey the erotic charge of interpenetrating light, space, force, and fluid.

Isidore's encyclopedic account of moon phases is another site of possible correspondence, and I have been dwelling on your postcard ever since it arrived. It leads me to consider whether even our most technical and instrumental interventions in the world (those of parchment book, astrological chart, quadrant, or digital image) can ever compass the rhythms outside. There is a conventional idea that technology alienates, but I wonder how lucid that thought really is, especially as machines facilitate the ease of our back-and-forth just now. I think of how Chaucer's *Treatise on the Astrolabe* sets out the procedure by which the "label shall than declare…at what houre of the day or of the night shall be flode…flode or ebbe, or halfe flode." Turning the dial to the right place on the device, intertidal activity practically becomes manifest on a circular metal plate. It is no small marvel. Spatiotemporal ebb and flow are indexed on a gadget that could be said to fix the flood but rather encourages a new sort of *fluency* with the ambient world.

The right words are hard enough to come by when we ignore our surroundings, discounting everything from birdsong to the chirrup of electronic devices as mere noise. For both of us, in these exchanges, the question is whether and how we can we attend better to more local phenomena. Let's acknowledge that all the human faculties (not just those associated with art and science, but also those required in everyday trade and technology) can and do discourse with things exterior to themselves. For do we not have many ways of "overhearing" the oceans? Various means of telling "stories" of the seas? There is no guarantee that our technical interfaces and conveyances (scientific or literary) will not end up fouling the waters. Many do. But more-than-human texts and technologies (conveniences that risk petrocidal ruin) are orientation devices, and there is an urgent need to recognize that orientation necessitates exposure.

This still sounds abstract and figurative perhaps, but what I think I'm saying in consonance with you is that we cannot always be sure where metaphors—abstracted figures like that stone and shell with which you began—begin and end. Can we ever know more? And where do we go from here?

A.

Four Swim Poems and a Picture

Steve Mentz

These four poems end this book as they gesture toward still-unnarrated waters. The poems ask what bodies learn from their encounters with Ocean. They are part of a larger project that explores swimming as an aesthetic practice for our age of ecological catastrophe.

The poems respond to this photograph by Vanessa Daws, a Dublin-based visual artist. The image was taken during "Lambay Swim," a collaborative journey made by the swimmers of Low Rock on 17th June 2014.

Image 1: Vanessa Daws, "Lambay Swim."

Elbow Above

As if in question an arm bends. Beneath,
Hidden by flood, a body. The angle marks
What it shows and conceals. Water ensheathes
Flesh. Wet, salt, and free-in-air, the arm arcs
Through two fluids by turns, unmarked.
What does the swimmer know of the sea?
Elbow promises a plunge we can't see,
The knife of re-entry, when landed flesh
Splits sea. No splash nor strain but repeated plea
That human form with ocean surge can mesh.

Six in a Boat

We are too many, sing the mariners, off-key.
Too many!

Up we go, and down the swell.
Too many!

In that carved-out space where wood displaces sea.
Too many!

We float and roll and row and watch and be.
Too many!

This is no way for land apes to live with flood.
Too many!

We round our backs above arcs through which we scud.
Too many!

Like music the oars keep time's splashing bell.
Too many!

Tuning salt ears to hear nor heaven nor hell.
Too many!

Invisible Bodies

Not nothing but everything
Spreads its bulk below. Globe-girdling, world-
Changing, moving, its wet fingers seep into
Any dry place you can name:
My body, these words, your face or hands or just-speaking
Mouth.
I have to believe it!
That the swimmer's body knows that greater body,
Not as you know a lover or a riddle or a problem in logic
But as things of opposite nature know one another
By imaginary subtraction, cross-formation, hidden
Additions.

Headless

Whatever he sees it's not through our air.
Light bends underwater.
It turns and diffracts, changes colors, closes distance.
Inside that slate-swell, the more-than-blue, all-shifting—
There is little he can see or think or do.
Might invisibility be his secret?
What is it like to swim headless,
Without thoughts or visions or sounds or smells?
No taste either: just one endless undifferentiated touch,
Swirling around one body within that larger body.
The swimmer knows something of the sea.
But he can't speak it because while he swims
His face angles down
Beneath the surface.

About the Contributors

Elizabeth Albert

Elizabeth Albert's paintings and works on paper have been exhibited nationally and are in the collections of the Butler Institute, the Naples Art Museum, and the International Museum of Collage, Assemblage, and Construction. She has received fellowships from the NEA/ Mid-Atlantic Arts Council, the Pollock-Krasner Foundation, Inc., and the MacDowell Colony. She is Associate Professor at St. Johns University where she teaches in the Department of Art and Design and the Institute for Core Studies. Her favorite Oceanic sites include Dead Horse Bay, Coney Island Creek, and Valentino Pier.

Jamie "Skye" Bianco

Jamie "Skye" Bianco, Clinical Assistant Professor in NYU's Department of Media, Culture and Communication, is a practice-based digital media theorist, activist and artist working on a multi-site ecological investigation of toxic yet inhabited waterscapes. She mixes images, sound, video, animation, and lyrical prose in multimodal, performative, web-based, computational/algorithmic and installation formats. Bianco also farms organic vegetables in the Catskills, advocating sustainable food, water and land use practices. She received a PhD in English from CUNY.

Jeffrey Jerome Cohen

Jeffrey Jerome Cohen, Professor of English at George Washington University, did not know that water would speak to him until this project opened New York to transit and conveyance instead of wandering on foot. He grew up and spent much of his life not far from the Charles River, with its pollution, swamps, and history, but his favorite waterways are after its flow empties into Boston Harbor and the Gulf of Maine. His most recent book is *Stone: An Ecology of the Inhuman* (2015).

Vanessa Daws

Vanessa Daws is a visual artist and avid open water swimmer based in Dublin. Her art investigates the drive to immerse oneself in water. Swimming, journey, encounter, conversation, film and publications together comprise her art practice in a process she describes as "Psychoswimography." Vanessa is currently on an Art in Science Residency at UCD, Dublin. In 2014 Vanessa was recipient of the Artist in the Community Award and created the "Lambay Swim" in collaboration with the sea swimming community from Malahide, Co Dublin.

Lowell Duckert

Lowell Duckert is assistant professor of English at West Virginia University, specializing in early modern literature, ecotheory, and environmental criticism. With Jeffrey Jerome Cohen, he is editor of *Elemental Ecocriticism: Thinking with Earth, Air, Water, and Fire* and *Ecomaterialism*, a special issue of *postmedieval: a journal of medieval studies*. He is currently writing a book on early modern waterscapes, desire, and more-than-human forms of textual and corporeal composition. Deception Pass and North Puget Sound remain his greatest influences.

Jonathan Hsy

Jonathan Hsy is Associate Professor of English at George Washington University, where he also is Founding Co-Director of the GW Digital Humanities Institute. He publishes, blogs, and tweets about translation, disability, media, diversity, curiosity, travel, and beauty. He remembers fondly growing up along the Pacific Ocean (Puget Sound and San Francisco Bay), but if he could have a second childhood he'd try the Mediterranean. Follow him at www.inthemedievalmiddle.com or on twitter: @JonathanHsy.

Granville Ganter

Granville Ganter teaches at St. John's University. His research focuses on early American literature and cultures of oratory. He is the author of *The Collected Speeches of*

Sagoyewatha, or Red Jacket. He is currently working on a biography of an early women lecturer of the 1820s, Anne Laura Clarke. He loves the Hudson river and the Atlantic ocean.

Anne Harris

Anne Harris is most energized in the company of fellow seekers of medieval and early modern phenomena. Paintings, artifacts, texts, and a host of other resplendent materials motivate her research and scholarship in and around the field of art history. Her new position as Vice President for Academic Affairs at DePauw University makes her treasure and champion the great and good work of collegiality and beautiful writing. The rooms and corridors of the Cloisters constitute the New York neighborhood where her imagination runs free. Her favorite ocean remains the Atlantic seen from the coast of Brittany in France, and experienced on the east coast of North Carolina.

Alison Kinney

Alison Kinney is the author of the "Object Lessons" book *Hood* (Bloomsbury Publishing, 2016). Her writing has appeared in *Hyperallergic, The Mantle, New Criticals, Narratively, Avidly, The New York Times, The Atlantic,* and other publications. Her New York is Flatbush, Brooklyn; her body of water is Porto Venere's Gulf of Poets, where a long blue swim restored her ability to walk

Dean Kritikos

Dean Kritikos is a poet, born and raised in New York City, who presently teaches Composition at St. John's University. The Atlantic Ocean is his favorite body of water—especially the portion of which he walks into and along from the powder-like sands of Wildwood, New Jersey. Dean has critical work published or forthcoming from *Lehigh Valley Vanguard* and *War Literature and the Arts*, as well as poetry and prose in *ATOMIC*, Lament for the Dead, *NYSAI*, and anthologies from Great Weather for MEDIA and Crack the Spine.

Steve Mentz

Steve Mentz is Professor of English at St. John's University in New York City. He writes about swimming, oceans, ecologies, Shakespeare, and literary culture. His most recent book is *Shipwreck Modernity: Ecologies of Globalization, 1550–1719* (2015). He swims most often in Long Island Sound and blogs at www.stevementz.com.

Allan Mitchell

J. Allan Mitchell grew up among the eelgrass, barnacles, gulls, mudflats, contaminated clams, creosote logs, and maritime debris in White Rock on Semiahmoo Bay, a moon-shaped basin spanning British Columbia, Canada, and Washington State, USA. He is Associate Professor of English at the University of Victoria and author of *Becoming Human: The Matter of the Medieval Child* (2014).

Julie Orlemanski

Julie Orlemanski is Assistant Professor of English at the University of Chicago. She is finishing her first book manuscript, "Symptomatic Subjects: Bodies, Signs, and Narratives in Late Medieval England," and looks forward to starting a new one, "Things without Faces: Prosopopoeia in Medieval Writing." She misses the green Atlantic and the glamorous Pacific, but Lake Michigan is not half-bad.

Nancy Nowacek

Nancy Nowacek is an artist whose work is rooted in the ecology of the everyday: the processes, codes, and habits of life. Her practice is focused on the uses of the body as relates to work, architecture and urban space. She has shown in New York, the Bay Area, Los Angeles, Canada and Europe. Nowacek teaches design and public practice and has an MFA in Social Practice from California College of Arts. She is certified in personal training and lives in Brooklyn. As of publication, she is still building Citizen Bridge.

Chris Piuma

Chris Piuma, who designed this book, grew up in a part of Bayside, Queens, which did not feel particularly close to a bay. He is a poet, a musician, and an Associate Director of punctum books. He writes this note within view of the Southeast Arm of Placentia Bay, Newfoundland.

Bailey Robertson

Bailey recently completed a Master of Arts degree in English at St. John's University. Her MA thesis considered critical feminist theories of eating and eating disorders, and used these theories to interrogate the work of Charlotte Brontë, Lewis Carroll, and Angela Carter. She is also interested in creative responses to ecological crisis, and more broadly, finding activist applications for literary study. Her favorite body of water is the Atlantic Ocean, in which she has misplaced several personal items that she is sure will turn up eventually.

Karl Steel

Karl Steel is associate professor of English at Brooklyn College and the Graduate Center, CUNY. His work on medieval animals includes *How to Make a Human: Animals and Violence in the Middle Ages* (2011), and essays on feral children, worms, biopolitics and hunting, spontaneous generation, vegetarian philosophers, and now, oysters. Even in Brooklyn, he is always with the seagray skies of the Pacific Northwest.

Matt Zazzarino

Matt Zazzarino is a graduate student at Emerson College, where he is pursuing an MFA in Fiction. His favorite body of water is the Sea Lion Pool at the Bronx Zoo, where you can find him barking, clapping, and clowning for tourists all year round. Admission is free on Wednesdays.

Marina Zurkow

Marina Zurkow is a media artist focused on near-impossible nature and culture intersections. She uses life science, materials, and technologies to foster intimate connections between people and non-human agents. Zurkow is a 2011 John Simon Guggenheim Memorial Fellow, and granted awards from the New York Foundation for the Arts, New York State Council for the Arts, the Rockefeller Foundation, and Creative Capital. She is on full time faculty at ITP / Tisch School of the Arts, and is represented by bitforms gallery. The Atlantic Ocean, the North Fork John Day River in Oregon, a sinkhole in West Texas, and a little quarry in Vermont are some of her favorite bodies of water.

Index of Bodies of Water